——POULTRY——
Breeds and Management
AN INTRODUCTORY GUIDE
—— DAVID SCRIVENER ——

POULTRY
Breeds and Management
AN INTRODUCTORY GUIDE
DAVID SCRIVENER

THE CROWOOD PRESS

First published in 2008 by
The Crowood Press Ltd
Ramsbury, Marlborough
Wiltshire SN8 2HR

www.crowood.com

British Library Cataloguing-in-Publication Data
A catalogue record for this book is available from the British Library.

ISBN 978 1 86126 994 2

Photographic Acknowledgements
Thanks are due to the following hatcheries who kindly provided
photographs of the following Commercial Hybrid breeds: *Black Rock* –
Peter Siddons of Muirfield Hatchery, Kinross, Scotland; *Hebden Black*, *Calder
Ranger* and *Speckledy* – David Evans of Cyril Bason (Stokesay) Ltd, Craven
Arms, Shropshire; Dominant CZ Hybrids – Meadowsweet Poultry, the UK
Agent, of Dominant CZ, Lazne Bohdanec, Czech Republic.

All of the remaining photographs in this book are credited to the late John
Tarren (David Scrivener Archive).

Frontispiece: Dark Brahma male.

Disclaimer
The author and the publisher do not accept any responsibility in any
manner whatsoever for any error or omission, nor any loss, damage, injury
or liability of any kind incurred as a result of the use of any of the
information contained in this book, or reliance upon it.

Typeset by Jean Cussons Typesetting, Diss, Norfolk

Printed and bound in Singapore by Craft Print International Ltd

Contents

Introduction

The pure breeds of chickens, bantams and turkeys covered in this book are part of our rural heritage. At least two of them, Asil and Dorkings, have existed over two thousand years, then there are quite a few that were clearly illustrated in seventeenth-century paintings. The main period during which today's 'historic' breeds emerged was between 1845 (when the first poultry show was held) and 1914. Although new colour varieties of recognized old breeds are still being created today, very few completely new breeds have been recognized since the 1950s, and many hobbyists are not convinced that they were good ideas.

Large-scale commercial egg and poultry meat production developed in America during the 1920s and 30s. This period saw rapid advances in equipment, such as very large incubators, and in our understanding of genetics, nutrition and disease control to make it possible. Initially, a few pure breeds were used for this production, White Leghorns dominating American egg production for example. Between 1935 and 1965 all pure breeds were replaced by 'hybrids' for commercial production. White egg-laying hybrids were still essentially White Leghorns, but were rather smaller and differed in other details from earlier White Leghorns, in days when poultry showing and poultry farming were related activities. At one time almost everyone with a fairly large garden had a pen of hens, and breeders used local poultry shows as a 'shop window' to advertise their stock to domestic poultry keepers. The changes in meat chickens were much more dramatic. Broiler hybrid chickens, many of which started from crosses between White Cornish and White Plymouth Rocks, are now very different from the standard versions of these breeds. They reach the required sizes for killing in less than half the time of any pure breed, which is why chicken is now the cheapest meat in the supermarket rather than the luxury it used to be.

There have been some interesting development in commercial hybrid breeding since the 1980s, such as naked-necked broilers for rearing in hot climates and layers of blue-shelled eggs for the free-range/organic sector, but it remains true to say that only a tiny minority of the main old pure breeds are represented in the secret breeding departments of the hybrid companies.

People who keep poultry as a hobby are in the fortunate position of not having to worry too much exactly how many eggs their hens lay, or how quickly their surplus cockerels grow because their birds are, in most cases, also family pets that happen to be useful and productive as well. They most probably start hen keeping because they have concerns about commercial egg production methods, but they usually end up having more eggs being laid than the family can eat, so their birds become an interest in themselves, not just a means to an end.

There is an ever increasing range of hybrids bred for organic producers and home poultry keepers that are given names that lead some confused beginners to think they are traditional breeds. This book is intended to remedy such confusion by describing all the real old breeds likely to be encountered by beginners. There are more old breeds, but they are so rare that most readers are unlikely to see them.

Those who live in places where cockerels are not a problem, or have enough space to keep chickens and turkeys, can transform their menagerie into a really useful conservation flock. Beginners usually buy a few pure breeds to add to their hybrids, but unfortunately (from a breed conservation perspective) many never really make the most of their houses and runs. Although this book does not have space for many of the rarest breeds, a lot of the varieties included here are currently being kept by only a handful of enthusiasts worldwide. Most breeds exist in several colour varieties in two size versions, large fowl and bantam (miniature). In many cases breeds are only regarded as popular because of the majority who keep the main colours, with other colours being very rare indeed.

All types of poultry, including commercial hybrids and cross-breds, can be productive and charming pets. The same can be said of pure breeds, especially rare pure breeds, but they also bring an extra dimension to your garden flock. Visiting, and eventually entering, poultry shows is the social side of the hobby. Only a small minority of poultry breeders are regular exhibitors at the major shows, a situation that is unlikely to greatly change. However, small local shows are held in many countries, in village halls or indoor riding centres in winter, as part of agricultural shows and other outdoor events in summer.

Everyone who keeps pure breeds of poultry should visit these events, where they will get to know the other people in their area with the same interests. As they look around these shows they will notice that while some of the birds present are perfectly prepared and manicured, many of the birds owned by regular exhibitors seem more like 'normal hens', clearly entered by people not much more expert than themselves. There will be some classes where none of the experts are competing, so wherever you live there are certain to be a lot of breeds that are like yours and that you can start showing with a good chance of winning locally.

Despite needing somewhere to keep your flock, hobby poultry breeding is an activity in which a huge range of people of all ages and incomes can participate. Senior citizens and teenagers have frequently won 'Show Champion' awards, having beaten millionaire competitors. Attention to detail is more important than wealth when the objects of everyone's attention are bantams small enough to sit in the palm of your hand.

Red Sussex by J.W. Ludlow, circa 1912.

──── 1 ────
What to Keep, and Where to Buy Them

Some enthusiastic beginners have a rapidly growing 'chicken town' of hen houses, with a different variety in each of them. This is not how it should be done. Almost all of the well-known people in our hobby limit themselves to a manageable total flock size, for the time and space they have available, and specialize in a few varieties, keeping quite a number of each. Trying a lot of different kinds may be a useful learning phase, but one to be passed through as quickly as possible. Hobbyists who are primarily interested in eggs, who might eventually enter the egg section of poultry shows, might settle down to one blue egg, one brown egg and one white egg breed. Others might have a favourite breed, perhaps one with local or family historical connections, and keep (where applicable) several colour varieties, large and bantam, of it.

How many birds do other hobbyists keep?

Everyone is different of course, but many fanciers keep about five male and fifteen adult breeding and showing birds of each variety over winter. They will hope to hatch and rear about thirty youngsters each spring. In late summer/early autumn they will kill some of the surplus males (on average, the thirty youngsters will be 15m:15f), and carefully decide which of the adults and better youngsters to keep through the following winter. Even well-known exhibitors, regular winners at the shows, do not have many customers for male birds. Sad as it may be, many are inevitably destined for the freezer. Pure breeds are traditionally sold in trios of a male and two females. They can be entered in poultry auctions or you can advertise in poultry and smallholding magazines, on the internet, in local newspapers or the notice-board at your local animal feed retailer (if it has one). It is essential that you sell, eat, give to friends, or otherwise reduce your flock over winter so there are enough empty hen houses for the next breeding season.

On this basis, a typical hobbyist with three breeds would have a total of sixty adult birds just before the breeding season, rising to about 150 in early autumn, and then gradually being reduced back down to sixty again. A single-breed specialist with the same total flock size may be able to keep more than three colour varieties as there are some cases where it is normal practice to cross colour varieties within a breed. A flock fluctuating between sixty and 150 might seem like a large amount to the less enthusiastic members of poultry-keeping families, and if the proposed birds are turkeys and the largest breeds of chickens, their alarm would probably be justified – that could be an expensive hobby. At the other extreme, a flock of 150 of the smaller bantam breeds can be comfortably accommodated in a surprisingly small area, and they won't eat that much either.

There are regulations concerning the sale of eggs to the public, in most countries with exemptions for small-scale hobbyists, but it would be wise to check on current regulations if you are likely to have a lot of eggs to sell.

How many birds do I need to breed annually?

Thirty has already been given as an average, but breeds differ in the quality and uniformity of the youngsters they produce. Some breeds are difficult to breed anyway, the most extreme being a very rare Japanese breed, the Yamato Gunkei. Sebright bantams are also notoriously infertile. Specialists of these two would be overjoyed if they managed to breed thirty in a season. Other breeds may be easy to breed as such, but could have a genetically unstable plumage pattern, comb shape or other feature. Lakenvelder chickens are in this category, and sixty or more would need to be bred annually to ensure ten worthy of showing or future breeding.

To remind you again, on average half of every batch of chicks will be males. If you would like to end the breeding season with a significant number of females for future laying (to keep or to sell) you probably need to incubate a lot more eggs than you think. Apart from all those males, not all of the eggs will be fertile, and not all of the fertile eggs will hatch.

Sources of stock

Apart from the 'Utility type' of some breeds, the most reliable source of pure breeds is through the poultry show scene. You can visit shows and meet the breeders personally, or be put in touch with them through breed club secretaries. These can be found via the main poultry websites on the internet, and poultry magazines include a list of them in at least one issue a year.

Some poultry shows have a sales section, usually a safe place to buy as the birds offered for sale will be from reliable breeders, plus there will be judges, show officials and experienced fanciers present to give a 'second opinion' on any birds you are thinking about. If the variety you would like to buy is only in the competitive classes, not the sales section, ask the show organizers to point out their owner(s). As the birds they are showing will probably be their best specimens, they are unlikely to be for sale, but he/she may have stock for sale at home, and a visit can be arranged for a later date. Large shows have a printed catalogue, with the names, addresses and phone numbers of almost all exhibitors – some who have suffered thefts ask not to be listed.

Advertisements in poultry and smallholding magazines, and poultry auctions (also advertised in the magazines) are the other main sources of stock. Whether visiting an advertiser or attending an auction, buyers need some breed and general poultry knowledge if they are to avoid buying a poor lot. Advertisers and auction vendors may range from leading experts to novice breeders who may be well-meaning but are actually selling grossly sub-standard birds. Any advertisers you visit who can say the birds for sale are bred from show winners should be OK.

Some auctioneers arrange judges to 'grade' all lots before the sale starts, which is a great help for confused beginners. Despite this guide, some lots go for much higher or much lower prices than most knowledgeable breeders would think they are worth. Taking large Wyandottes as an example breed, poorly marked specimens of the Laced, Partridge and Silver Pencilled varieties still look pretty to bidders who don't know the details of the breed standard, so often sell for high prices. Conversely, excellent Black Wyandottes may go cheaply because black chickens do not seem to appeal to many beginners nowadays. If in doubt, look around the crowd for people wearing poultry-club badges who might be able and willing to help.

As most breeders are hobbyists, not many will be able or willing to sell groups of females without males as they do not want to kill more males than they already have to for the selling of trios rather than pairs. Two of the Autosexing Breeds, the brown-egg-laying Welbar and the blue-egg-laying Crested Legbar, are gradually becoming more popular as a 'second breed' with fanciers who can identify and kill cockerel chicks, and then rear pullets for sale to cover the costs of their main showing breed.

Buying hatching eggs

If you have an incubator this can be a cost-effective way of starting with a breed. Some competitive show exhibitors do not sell hatching eggs, but many with rarer varieties prefer any eggs they cannot incubate themselves to be hatched by someone else rather than be eaten.

Some breeders charge relatively high prices for hatching eggs, but replace (free) infertile eggs. Others follow the simpler path of selling at lower prices but not guaranteeing anything beyond the fact that the cockerel was definitely in the pen with his mates. They will still charge a bit more than eating egg prices as the eggs will have been selected for ideal size, shape and shell colour/quality for incubation.

Indian Game Bantams by J.W. Ludlow, 1899. Compare the taller, less broad-bodied type they were then with Indian Game Bantams as they are now, and have been since about 1950, as in the photo on page 43.

2

Chicken and Bantam Breeds

This chapter covers all breeds likely to be available to a beginner, although not all of them are bred everywhere. For details of the rarest breeds, see *Rare Poultry Breeds* (David Scrivener, The Crowood Press). Many rare breeds, and even rare colour varieties of otherwise popular breeds, are only bred by a handful of enthusiasts world-wide, so will be difficult to locate or buy.

Breeds are described in alphabetical order, with the large and bantam versions of each breed together; they are, after all, identical in all respects except size. After an initial period of trying several breeds, many hobbyists decide to specialize in just one breed, but with several colour varieties and both size versions of them.

Some historical details are given of all the breeds, after all one of the reasons people keep pure breeds is to conserve a little piece of rural history. Many people keep the breed associated with their locality.

The Poultry Club of Great Britain divides breeds into groups for the purposes of section awards at shows, similar to the way dog shows are divided into Hound, Terrier and other groups. The sections are given after each breed name, and are a general indication of what they are like. The sections are:

Hard-Feather Large Fowl and Hard-Feather Bantam These are the old fighting cock breeds (Asil, Old English Game, Shamo), related exhibition breeds (Ko-Shamo, Malay, Modern Game) and Indian Game/Cornish, an exhibition and meat breed.

Heavy Soft-Feather Large Fowl and Heavy Soft-Feather Bantam Most heavy breeds were once either table breeds or dual-purpose farm breeds. Heavy-breed bantams are the miniature versions of their large counterparts, having the same characteristics on a small scale. Heavy breeds are popular with beginners as they are generally docile and easy to handle, and the hens go broody to hatch their own chicks.

Light Soft-Feather Large Fowl and Light Soft-Feather Bantam Most are active birds that were originally developed for egg production. Apart from Silkies, they seldom go broody.

True Bantam These are bantam-only breeds, with no large fowl equivalent. UK standard Pekins are almost, but not quite, the same as Cochin Bantams in other countries.

Rare Breed, Large Fowl and Bantam A UK definition, based on the breeds covered by our Rare Poultry Society, not having their own breed club here. If a rare breed becomes more popular, and a new breed club is formed, it then joins whichever of the above sections is applicable. The equivalent US organization, the Society for the Preservation of Poultry Antiquities (SPPA), has a slightly different list of breeds. Obviously some American breeds are rarer in the UK, and some British breeds are rarer in the USA.

ANCONA (LIGHT SOFT-FEATHER, LARGE FOWL AND BANTAM)

The ancestors of this breed came from the region around the city of Ancona on the north-east coast of Italy, but these were farmyard fowls in an assortment of plumage colours. They were made into a standard breed, in just one colour variety, black with a white tip on each feather, by a succession of English breeders between 1850 and 1890. It took a long time to achieve the neat, evenly distributed white spotting they have now. Ancona bantams were first made in Yorkshire, about 1900, about the same time as the rare rose-combed version.

Anconas have a reputation for being wild and nervous; when panicked they can easily fly over normal hen run fences. This has limited their popularity, but this highly developed survival instinct is a real advantage in free-range flocks in areas where foxes or other predators are a problem. Ancona hens are good layers and hardly ever go broody. Ancona chicks intended for showing should be handled and petted as much as possible to make them as tame as possible.

They are a typical light breed in general shape and size, with weights ranging from 2kg (4½lb) pullets up to 3kg (6½lb) adult cocks

Ancona female.

for the large fowl and an equivalent of 510g (18oz) to 680g (24oz) for bantams. Although essentially a laying breed, surplus large Ancona cockerels are quite compact and meaty for their size. The normal single comb on Anconas should be upright on males, flopping over on females, with the rarer rose-combed variety ideally having a compact, close to the skull comb formation, as seen on Wyandottes. Ear lobes are white; shanks and feet are yellow with black spots. The white spots on the plumage should be quite small, as evenly distributed as possible and V-shaped, not round. The spots get bigger and more numerous with each adult moult, so an under-spotted first-year bird will probably be correctly marked for showing the following year, whereas a correctly marked first-year bird may be over-spotted in its second year, almost certainly so in its third year. As with other breeds that have a limited show life, they can be bred from and will continue laying as long as any other breed. Do not be alarmed by their juvenile plumage, a penguin-like arrangement of white breast and black back; they will moult into the expected pattern as they reach maturity. A new blue with white spots variety has been developed in Germany and The Netherlands.

ANDALUSIAN (RARE BREED, LARGE FOWL AND BANTAM)

This breed had a very similar history to Anconas, a standard breed

15

made from an assortment of farmyard fowls, this time imported from the Andalusia region of Spain. John Taylor, who lived in the Shepherd's Bush area of London, was a prominent breeder in the transformation of both Anconas and Andalusians into standard breeds in the 1850s. A few of the birds he and his friends started with were a bluish grey shade with an indistinct darker edging to each feather. Specialist livestock artists, such as Joseph Williamson Ludlow (whose pictures are now collector's items), painted idealized versions, with a beautifully even blue-grey ground colour and wonderfully sharp black lacing. It was many years before fanciers were able to turn the birds in the pictures into a living reality. Only 50 per cent of the chicks bred from a pen of Andalusians are blue at all (*see below*), and of these not all have the ideal even ground colour or perfect lacing. Andalusian bantams were first recorded about 1880. The difficulties of breeding really good Andalusians has limited their popularity.

The general body shape and size is similar to Anconas and several other light breeds. Andalusians have a single comb, dark-coloured eyes and white ear lobes. All plumage should be bluish grey with black lacing except for neck feathering of both sexes and the saddle hackles of males, which are glossy bluish black.

Andalusians, pair. The male was still winning prizes at shows, despite its faulty, almost white, tail feather. Judges allow for the difficulty of breeding perfect specimens of this breed.

The 'blue' plumage is caused by an incompletely dominant gene that restricts the formation of black pigment. Blues have one of these genes present, and birds with two of these genes are nearly white, with a few random blue and black markings. They are called 'Splashes'. Birds that are completely black are also bred in some of the possible matings listed below. All Andalusian breeders have stuck to the tradition that only Blues are shown, never Blacks or Splashes, even though both can be useful for breeding.

Blue × Blue → 50% Blue, 25% Black, 25% Splash

Black × Splash → 100% Blue

Blue × Black → 50% Blue, 50% Black

Blue × Splash → 50% Blue, 50% Splash

Black × Black → 100% Black

Splash × Splash → 100% Splash

All these matings (except the last two) might be of use, depending on the birds you have.

APPENZELLER SPITZHAUBEN (RARE BREED)

These pretty chickens with pointed feather crests and horned combs are from the Appenzell Canton of north-eastern Switzerland. Although they have probably existed in their homeland for over 300 years, Appenzeller Spitzhaubens have only been bred in the UK since the 1970s. There are several colour varieties of Appenzeller Spitzhaubens: Silver Spangled, Gold Spangled, Chamois Spangled, Barred, Black, Black-Mottled and Blue. There was a (now extinct) British breed, the Yorkshire Hornet, that was very similar to Gold Spangled Appenzeller Spitzhaubens. It is not known if they were directly related. Appenzeller Spitzhauben bantams were made about 1990, but as large Spitzhaubens only weigh from 1.3kg (3lb) pullets up to 2kg (4½lb) for the adult cocks, the bantams would have to be really tiny to be distinctive and interesting.

They are active foraging birds that need free range or runs with very high fences, preferably covered over to form aviaries. If it is intended to show them, they need a lot of handling throughout their growing period to become tame enough to face a judge and the viewing public. If allowed to, they often perch up in trees instead of roosting in houses. Even with their acute survival instincts this is not a good idea, so train them to come in by giving an evening feed in

Gold Spangled Appenzeller Spitzhauben male.

Silver Spangled Appenzeller Spitzhauben female.

their house, and shut them in. The hens are reasonably good layers of white eggs.

ARAUCANA, RUMPLESS AND BRITISH TYPES AND AMERAUCANA (LIGHT S.F. BREED)

Since about 1970 these have gone from being an obscure rarity to a popular favourite with hobbyist poultry keepers, the blue, turquoise or olive green-shelled eggs being their interesting aspect. There are even commercial producers of coloured eggs using Araucanas and Crested Legbars (*see* Autosexing Breeds) to breed commercial blue-egg layers.

Chile is usually given as their country of origin, but the first Spanish explorers of South America reported them all over the continent. As all domestic chickens were presumed to have been developed from the species of Jungle Fowl, all of which are wild in south-east Asia, the well-documented existence of (unusual) domestic chickens in South America this long ago was a scientific mystery. Recent research indicates that they were brought across the Pacific Ocean, island by island, in ancient times.

With their long history spread over many countries, it is not surprising that there are several type of Araucana. Rumpless Araucanas, some of which have beards, and some of which have unique feathered 'ear tufts', are considered to be the true original type by some, but not all, experts. The British-type Araucana and the American Ameraucana are standardized forms of more 'normal' blue-egg-laying chickens. There are large and bantam versions of all three types.

Blue-red British-type Araucana male. Ameraucanas are similar, except they do not have the small crest behind the comb of the British type.

Lavender British-type Araucana bantam female.

19

Black-red Rumpless Araucana male.

Both British-type Araucanas and American Ameraucanas are hardy, medium-sized breeds, the hens being good layers and surplus cockerels making a fine roast chicken. They are virtually identical in general shape and size, both have pea combs and beards, the only difference being that the British type also has a modest-sized feathered head crest, absent on Ameraucanas. All three types can be obtained in several colour varieties, including: Black-red, Blue-red, Black, White and Blue. In British-type Araucanas the most popular colour variety is the Lavender.

ASIL (HARD FEATHER)

This fighting cock breed from India is very aggressive, and certainly not suitable for beginners. It is included in this chapter only because it is the most ancient breed in the world, mentioned in a document written in 1280BCE. Asil are only kept by historically minded enthusiasts.

AUSTRALORP (HEAVY SOFT FEATHER, LARGE AND BANTAM)

The first Black Orpingtons (*see* Orpington) were more like today's Australorps. Orpingtons became a fluffy show breed in the UK, but some of the original type had been exported to Australia and other parts of the old British Empire, where they had remained a practical

Asil male. These muscular birds with tight-fitting plumage are heavier than they look. Details of their plumage colour are not considered important, greater emphasis being on body shape, low tail carriage, light eye colour, compact pea comb and natural complete absence of wattles on both sexes.

Black Australorp trio. Ideally they should have black eyes and red faces – a difficult combination to achieve, especially on females. Red-faced pullets often have lighter eye colour, and black-eyed pullets often have dark facial skin.

farm breed. In 1921 some 'Australian Black Orpingtons', soon shortened to Australorps, were brought back to England.

As a hobbyists' breed, Black Australorps of both sizes are easy to keep, easy to get ready for showing by beginners not yet skilled in the art of show preparation, good layers, good broodies and mothers, and surplus cockerels (even the bantams) are plump and meaty. They are a neat and tidy-looking breed, and their glossy greenish black plumage looks wonderful against green grass when they are running out in the sun. White and Blue Australorps are both very recently made colour varieties.

At first glance they are a very straightforward looking chicken, and a beginner seeing a large class of them at a show would think them all identical, however there are a lot of fine details in shape and headpoints that separate the best from the rest. This is best understood by asking an expert to explain the finer points at a show, where you can compare them closely.

AUTOSEXING BREEDS – CRESTED LEGBAR, LEGBAR, RHODEBAR, WELBAR

(Rare Breeds, Large Fowl and Bantams of some) Other Autosexing Breeds are rare or extinct.

Autosexing breeds have the very useful characteristic of having different coloured male and female chicks. Although the colours vary from one Autosexing Breed to another, within each breed the males are always lighter than the females. If large numbers are being hatched, the majority of the cockerel chicks can be killed at day-old to reduce rearing costs.

Most of this group of breeds were developed at Cambridge University's Agricultural Research Department by Professor R.C. Punnett and Michael Pease. They started in the 1920s, and launched their first Autosexing Breed, the Cambar, at the 1930 World Poultry Congress, an event held every three years or so to enable poultry farmers and scientists studying poultry to get together. Later trends in large-scale poultry meat and egg production, including the development of hybrids, meant that Autosexing Breeds never became as economically important as a lot of people thought they would in the 1930s. Read *Rare Poultry Breeds* (David Scrivener, The Crowood Press) for full details of all Autosexing Breeds.

The plumage patterns of Autosexing Breeds are pretty, but rather too fuzzy and indistinct to interest many show exhibitors, although two of them, Cream/Crested Legbars and Welbars have been bred in large numbers since about 2000 for back garden hen keepers.

Cream or Crested Legbar. Araucanas were crossed with Gold Legbars (*see below*) to create this breed, which is becoming very popular because, like Araucanas, it lays blue eggs. It was made by accident in the course of studying its unusual diluted plumage colour pattern, the team at Cambridge never dreaming that one day it would become the most commercially important of all the Autosexing Breeds. See the blue eggs at your local supermarket.

Gold and Silver Legbars. These two colour varieties were made during the Second World War from crosses of Barred Rocks, Brown Leghorns and White Leghorns. They were expected to be commercially important laying breeds after the War, but American hybrids were better layers. They are very rare now, but are pretty and are fairly good layers of white eggs.

Rhodebar male. The barring is clear on males, rather blurred and indistinct on females.

Welbar bantam female.

Rhodebar. As Rhode Island Reds were one of the most commercially important breeds from the 1930s until the 1950s, it is not surprising that an Autosexing version would be made. A team of agricultural scientists in Canada made one strain in the 1940s, and two private breeders in Essex, England, made another strain in the 1950s. Both strains were large, but a recently made bantam version still exists in the UK, but these are very rare.

Welbar. This Welsummer-based Autosexing Breed was made by a Mr Humphreys from Devon. He started in 1941, taking until about 1950 to get their plumage colours stable enough for the difference in male and female chick colours to be reliable. A bantam version was made in the 1980s by Bristol-based fancier, John Buck. Both large and bantam Welbars lay the same dark brown eggs as Welsummers, so they are likely to become more popular than ever before.

BARBU D'ANVERS OR ANTWERP BELGIAN (TRUE BANTAM)

Similar bantams can be seen in seventeenth-century paintings, but they were not made into a proper breed with an agreed standard until Belgian fanciers formed a breed club and started to show them *circa* 1895–1905. A group of Belgian fanciers entered some in the 1911, 1912 and 1913 Crystal Palace Shows in London, resulting in a British Belgian Bantam Club being formed in 1915. They were slow to become very popular here, but now fine displays of Barbu d'Anvers can be seen at even the smallest local shows in England. Although it takes some skill and years of selective breeding to produce a show winner, they are one of the best of the tiny true Bantam breeds for beginners to try.

Barbu d'Anvers are jaunty little birds with a short back and prominent breast. Their wings are carried low, with the tips pointing to the ground, and the tail feathers of cocks should be sabre-shaped, not curving in a semi-circle like most other breeds. They have a rose comb, which should be compact and close to the skull – high, oddly shaped combs being a common fault. Under the beak is a feathery beard. They sometimes peck each other's beards, especially in the moulting season. It may be necessary to isolate some birds at this time.

All the Belgian Bantam breeds are available in a huge range of pretty colours and patterns. The Quail plumage pattern is particularly associated with Belgian Bantams, and there are four colour versions of it: Normal Quail, Blue Quail, Lavender Quail and Silver Quail. Normal Quails can be crossed with any of the other three variants, but crossing among these three results in a genetic mix-up.

Quail Barbu d'Anvers (UK and Belgium)/Quail Antwerp Belgian (USA) female.

There are also Black, Black-Mottled, Blue, Blue-Mottled, Cuckoo, Lavender and White varieties.

BARBU DU GRUBBE (TRUE BANTAM)

This is a rumpless (tailless) version of Barbu d'Anvers, and it is identical to them in every way, except for the tail. They appeared as a mutation in the flock belonging to Robert Pauwels, one of the 1895 founders of Belgian Bantams. Barbu du Grubbe are much rarer than Barbu d'Anvers.

BARBU D'UCCLES (TRUE BANTAM)

This breed is very closely related to the Booted Bantam (*see below*), a relationship that has caused some confusion, especially in America. The most popular colour variety of the breed, the Millefleurs (French for thousand flowers), is often mistakenly thought to be the breed's name.

Barbu d'Uccles were established as a separate breed from Booteds in Belgium in 1905. In Germany and The Netherlands Bearded Booteds are also standardized, but they do not have the distinctive neck feather formation, the 'boule' of Barbu d'Uccles. The most popular colour varieties are Millefleurs (golden-brown with black spangles and white tips), Porcelaine (the same pattern diluted to cream and lavender) and Black-Mottled. Blue-Millefleurs (light golden-brown and blue) is a new colour version of the same pattern.

Millefleurs Barbu d'Uccles (UK and Belgium)/Bearded Millefleurs Booted (USA) pair.

25

Barbu d'Uccles have beards, the boule feather formation at the back of the neck, a single comb and heavily feathered legs and feet. The foot feathering is quite brittle and easily broken, plus it must be kept clean for showing. This all needs special care, so only those beginners prepared to follow advice given by expert breeders should try them. Millefleurs and Porcelaine Barbu d'Uccles are routinely mated together, which improves the colours of both varieties.

BARBU D'EVERBERG (TRUE BANTAM)

This is a rare rumpless (tailless) version of Barbu d'Uccles, also developed by Robert Pauwels in Belgium *circa* 1900.

BARBU DE WATERMAEL (TRUE BANTAM)

These cute little bantams were created by father and son, Antoine and Oscar Dresse, who lived in Watermael-Bosvoorde, a suburb of Brussels, Belgium. Although first exhibited at the 1922 Brussels Show, they were not regularly seen in the UK until the 1970s.

They are smaller than Barbu d'Anvers, but are similar in general shape and style. They also have feathery beards, the major difference being their unique headgear, a rose comb with three rear spikes, and behind that a feathered crest. Colour varieties are as Barbu d'Anvers.

Blue Barbu de Watermael female.

Barnevelder pair.

BARNEVELDER (HEAVY SOFT FEATHER, LARGE AND BANTAM)

Barneveld, a town in the middle of The Netherlands, is the tradi-tional centre of the Dutch poultry industry. It has a large wholesale egg market, an agricultural college that specializes in poultry, and now there is also a poultry museum. Development of the Barn-evelder breed began in the 1880s, when various local chickens were crossed with Langshans, with Gold Laced Wyandottes being added to the mixture about 1900. After a lot of selective breeding to make them into a uniform new breed, they were launched at the World Poultry Congress at Den Haag (The Hague) in 1921. Mrs J.M. Walker was impressed by them at The Congress, and arranged the first international consignment by aeroplane of day-old chicks to bring them to England soon afterwards.

Barnevelder Bantams were first made (independently) by fanciers in England, Germany and The Netherlands in the 1930s, but these strains did not lay brown eggs, and died out during the Second World War anyway. New, better strains were made in the 1950s and 1960s.

The main colour variety of Barnevelders is the Double Laced, a combination of glossy black and mahogany that can only be fully appreciated when a flock is running outside in the sun. Males are slightly different in Britain from those in The Netherlands; they have laced breast feathering in the UK, and are solid black in The Nether-lands. There is a pretty new variety, with the same Double Laced pattern, but with the black changed to blue. Other colours of Barn-evelders have included Black, Partridge, Silver Double Laced and white, but they are very rare or extinct.

Barnevelders are practical and attractive birds, and both the large and bantam versions would be an ideal choice for beginners, whether it is intended to show them or not. They are easy to prepare for showing.

BOOTED OR SABELPOOT (RARE TRUE BANTAM)

Some of the first bantams imported to Europe from Java in the sixteenth century had feathered legs and feet, and this feature was emphasized by Belgian, Dutch, English and German fanciers over the following centuries until some birds had extraordinarily profuse and long 'footings'. British fanciers neglected Booted in favour of Barbu d'Uccles for many decades, but Booteds have become more popular again since the 1990s. Many strains in the UK have been imported from The Netherlands, hence the common use of their Dutch name here, Sabelpoot. Huge numbers of them, in a wide range of colour varieties, can be seen at the major Dutch and German poultry shows.

Booteds are normal bantams in every way except for their leg and foot feathering. They need houses that are large enough for them to be kept inside comfortably when it is wet outside. If it is intended to show them, they will need a lot of show preparation and extra care, so they are not suitable for most beginners to show. Even when kept just as garden pets, they still need suitable housing – a Booted Bantam with its foot feathers caked in mud is a sorry sight.

They have a small single comb and red ear lobes. Their main feature is obviously their feathered legs and feet, which start with long 'vulture hocks', a clump of long, stiff feathers that grow out from the hock joint (the joint between the scaled part and feathered

White Booted (UK and USA)/Sabelpoot (Netherlands) male. This front view shows the great length of foot feathers that can only be maintained with special care and housing.

part of the leg), pointing down and to the rear. Feathers should grow out between the scales of the shanks and outer and middle toes, these to be as long and profuse as possible. Colour varieties include: Black, Blue, Buff, Lavender, White, Black-Mottled, Blue-Mottled, Buff-Mottled, Millefleurs, Porcelaine, Citron-Millefleurs, Blue-Millefleurs, Silver-Millefleurs, Columbian, Barred, Black-Red/Partridge, Duckwing. Not all varieties are available in all countries.

BRAHMA (HEAVY SOFT FEATHER, LARGE AND BANTAM)

Large Brahmas, along with their close relations, Cochins, are two of the most fantastic-looking breeds of exhibition poultry, both being massive birds that look even more massive because of their very profuse body, leg and foot feathering. They were developed by American and British breeders from 'Shanghaes' imported from northern China in the mid-nineteenth century. The original imports had less foot feathering and variable plumage markings.

Some of these imports had various combinations of black and white feathering, and these were first called 'Grey Shanghaes'. The name Brahma was invented (initially 'Brahma-Pootra') after a river in India by Dr Kerr of Philadelphia in 1849. He is said to have stuck some pins in a map of Asia until he found a name that sounded suitably exotic – this breed had no real connection to anywhere in India. Another early Brahma breeder was George Burnham of Roxbury, Massachusetts, who sent nine birds to Queen Victoria, with as much publicity as he could arrange.

Although several more colour varieties of Brahmas have been made since the 1970s, for most of the time since 1850 there were just two: Dark and Light. Dark Brahma males have black breast, leg and tail feathering, with the neck and saddle hackles being white with black striping. Dark females are 'Pencilled', with fine light and dark grey concentric lines within each feather. Both sexes of Light Brahmas are white in all parts expects for black neck striping, wing markings and tail feathers. The first of the newer colour varieties were Golds and Buff Columbians, with gold replacing white in the Dark and Light patterns. Even newer are blue (instead of black) versions of Dark, Light, Gold and Buff Columbian patterns.

Despite their immense size, Brahmas are very docile birds and are popular pets. They need large houses so they can be kept inside when it is wet and muddy outside, and they eat a lot. Brahmas will often sleep on the floor of their houses, so perches are not necessary,

Dark Brahma male.

Dark Brahma female. These have exactly the same colours and markings as Silver Pencilled Wyandottes, the historically different names for a single plumage pattern no doubt being confusing for beginners to our hobby. Conversely (or perversely?), Dark Dorkings are completely different in colour and markings.

but the floor must be covered with clean wood shavings, and the house secure and rat-proof.

Brahma Bantams were first made by W.F. Entwisle of Wakefield, Yorkshire, 1870–90. Entwisle, and his son and daughter, were the first to make bantam versions of several breeds. Their much smaller size means they are easier to house, cheaper to feed, and are generally a more practical proposition than their large relations.

BRAKEL (RARE BREED)

These are rare everywhere in the world except for their homeland, the area around the village of Brakel and the market town of Aalst to the west of Brussels in Belgium. They are very similar to the Campine, originally from the area north of Brussels. Brakels are heavier than Campines, and are bred in the same two colour varieties, Gold and Silver versions of their characteristic barred pattern with a clear (silver or gold) neck. Brakel males have clear saddle hackles, whereas Campine males are 'hen feathered', with barred backs like the females of both breeds. Because the females of both breeds are so similar, with the danger of accidental cross-breeding, it is not a good idea to keep both Brakels and Campines.

CAMPINE (RARE BREED)

As indicated above, Campines originated in the area between Brussels and the border with The Netherlands. In their homeland they were bred with normal cock-feathered males, so making them identical with Brakels except for their slimmer build. Hen-feathered males had sometimes appeared, but the Belgian farmers killed them for the table. It was the British breeders who took Campines up

Silver Brakel male.

Silver Campine male.

31

about 1900 who decided to adopt hen-feathered males as their ideal for showing. Being quite rare, it may not be easy to find stock, but they would be an interesting breed for any beginner who seriously wants to help in the conservation of historic breeds. They lay white eggs, and are a typical active light breed in general temperament. Their plumage pattern is very distinctive, the feathers of all parts except the neck being barred, either black and white or black and gold. Most birds with good barring, especially on the upper breast, have a few black neck feathers that should gently be removed for showing.

COCHIN (HEAVY SOFT FEATHER)

Like Brahmas, Cochins did not come from their nominal place of origin either. Cochin-China was a French colony in what is now the southern part of Vietnam. Some very large chickens, but without feathered feet, were imported from there in 1843. The ancestors of present-day Cochins, then with modest foot feathering, were imported from Shanghai in northern China in 1849. Poultry experts called them 'Shanghaes', but ordinary poultry keepers had got used to the name 'Cochins' for all big feathery chickens from Asia. The increase in amount of foot feathering, and stabilization of plumage colours and patterns, was achieved by about 1880. The main colour varieties of Cochins are Black, Blue, Buff, Partridge and White. They are very similar to Brahmas in terms of docility, housing and feeding needs, foot feather care, and so on.

See Pekin Bantam for Cochin Bantams.

Buff Cochin male.

*Partridge Cochin
female.*

DORKING (HEAVY SOFT FEATHER, LARGE AND BANTAM)

Columella, a Roman writer, described plump chickens with a distinctive extra hind toe on each foot in the south of England 2,000 years ago. They were certainly the ancestors of the Dorking breed, although they were probably not identical to Dorkings of today. For most of their very long history they were considered the finest table birds in the world. They started to lose ground in this respect by about 1900, when breeders started to concentrate on plumage colour and other fancy points at the expense of practical considerations.

Dorkings were only kept going by a handful of enthusiasts for most of the twentieth century, but since the 1980s they have become much more popular here in the UK. During the long time that Dorkings were very rare, they inevitably suffered from the effects of inbreeding. Most of them looked OK, but when handled were revealed not to be as meaty as they should be. Today's Dorking Club members are trying to improve them.

Dorking Bantams have been known since 1890, but have always been very rare. A few more people have started keeping them since 2000, but there are still very few sources of stock. There are no great difficulties in breeding and exhibiting Dorking Bantams, so a beginner could soon become one of the leading Dorking Bantam breeders.

They have fairly short legs that, combined with their long back and large tail, gives them a generally horizontal appearance that has been called 'boat-shaped'. There are five colour varieties: Red, Silver Grey, Dark (once called 'Coloured'), Cuckoo and White. For historical reasons, the first two are only allowed single combs, the last two

Silver Grey Dorking male. The same plumage colour and pattern is called Silver Duckwing in the game breeds and Silver Partridge in Dutch bantams.

only rose combs, and Darks can have either type of comb. You may not be able to find the bantams in all five colours. Large Dorkings should be very large birds indeed, and even though many are not as heavy as their ancestors, they also have a long tail. They therefore need large houses, with perches well away from the house wall. The hens need extra large nest boxes. This is to reduce the chances of their tail feathers getting broken. Both sizes of Dorkings need outside runs to help keep them fit and active. These runs should be shaded (under trees perhaps) for Silver Greys and Whites to prevent them going brassy (*see* Glossary).

DUTCH (TRUE BANTAM)

Dutch Bantams, 'Hollandse Kriel' in their homeland, are very conventional in that they have a normal single comb, normal white ear lobes, are of normal shape with no unusual features like feathered feet or a crest, and come in a wide range of conventional plumage colours and patterns. They are unusually small however, with adult cocks having a maximum permitted weight of 550g (19½oz), and pullets only weighing 400g (14oz). They are ideal for those with small gardens.

Similar bantams have probably been bred in The Netherlands since the sixteenth century, but they were not officially standardized there until 1906, and a breed club was not formed for them until 1946. One of the leading fanciers in the process of refining them in size, breed points and plumage colours and patterns was Cornelis

Gold Partridge Dutch Bantam. This plumage colour and pattern is called Black-red/Partridge on most breeds in the UK, and 'Brown' on Leghorns. The British Dutch Bantam Club decided to follow direct translations of variety names used in The Netherlands.

S.Th. Van Gink (1890–1968), who was a specialist artist of poultry and fancy pigeon breed prints. They were a Rare Breed in the UK until 1982, when the Dutch Bantam Club was formed here. Since then, they have become more popular than many more established breeds.

Apart from their small size, their other great appeal is the range of colour varieties available: Gold Partridge, Silver Partridge, Yellow Partridge, Blue-Gold Partridge, Blue-Silver Partridge, Blue-Yellow Partridge, Crele, Cuckoo, Pile, Black, Blue, Lavender and White.

Although at first glance they seem a very simple breed, there are many fine details to be understood if you are to win with Dutch at the shows. These are best explained by an expert at a show where there are a lot of Dutch on display, to compare the best with the rest.

FAVEROLLES (HEAVY SOFT FEATHER, LARGE AND BANTAM)

Faverolles is a village south-west of Paris and south of the market town of Houdan, home of the Houdan breed (*see below*). When Shanghaes (*see* Brahmas and Cochins, *above*) became available to farmers in the mid-nineteenth century they were crossed with existing local breeds, in this area, the Houdan, to make new breeds. At first they were obviously a variable mixture of crossbreds, but wholesale poultry dealers supplying Paris soon called them Faverolles to distinguish them from pure Houdans. By the time some of them were imported to England in 1892 or 1893, they had really become uniform enough to be a proper new breed. Although never as popular in England as our Sussex breed, quite a few producers used to breed table chickens by crossing Faverolles hens with Indian Game cocks – the hybrid broilers of their day. Faverolles are still heavy and meaty birds, some cocks weighing over 5kg (11lb).

Their miniature version is quite large as well, some only just fitting in a normal bantam show cage. This puts them out of winning 'Best in Show' under most judges, despite the argument put forward by specialists that it was intended to keep Faverolles Bantams big enough for them to still be a useful layer and table bird – which they certainly are.

Large Faverolles are really massive, and the miniature version have the same build on a reduced scale. They have retained the beards and extra hind toe of their Houdan ancestors, but unlike Houdans, Faverolles have a small single comb and no crest. Faverolles have lightly feathered feet, similar to the original Shanghaes.

The most popular colour variety of Faverolles is the Salmon. Salmon males have a black beard, breast, underparts and tail. Their neck and saddle is straw colour and the back is mahogany. Salmon females have a light wheaten-brown neck, back and wings, with the remainder being a delicate creamy shade. Colour details of this variety are slightly different in England, France, Germany and the USA, so the relevant poultry breed standards books should be closely studied in all countries. Other colour varieties of Faverolles are Black, Blue, Buff, Cuckoo, Ermine (as Light Sussex) and White.

Salmon Faverolles male.

Chamois Pencilled Friesians, pair. Their colour tends to fade during summer, 'bleached' by sunlight. Shaded runs, with trees perhaps, help to minimize this effect.

FRIESIAN (RARE BREED)

This is an ancient breed from Friesland, the north-western province of The Netherlands. They are a small breed, a result of them originally being expected to forage around the fields and farmyards for most of their own food. Since they were introduced to the UK about 1990, large Friesians have often been entered in Rare Breed Bantam classes at shows by mistake. There are Friesian Bantams as well, but they are very tiny, similar in size to Dutch Bantams. Eight colour varieties are standardized in their homeland, but only Chamois Pencilled have been seen in the UK so far (2007). Males are golden-buff, as even as possible, except for their white fail feathers. These feathers should ideally have a fine golden-buff edging, but the edging is seldom complete or regular, so don't worry if your cock-erel is not perfect in this respect, no one else's will be either. Females have delicate white markings in an 'ears of wheat' design on golden-buff ground colour.

As Friesians have been active foraging chickens for well over 1,000 years it would be cruel to keep them inside or in small runs. They either need free-range conditions or large outside runs, preferably netted over the top to create an aviary. Normal hen-run fences will not keep them in.

FRIZZLE (HEAVY SOFT FEATHER, LARGE AND BANTAM)

The frizzle characteristic, feathers that curl out from the body, is caused by a single gene. Frizzled versions of Japanese (Chabo) Bantams and Polands (large and bantam) are recognized sub-varieties of those breeds all over the poultry-keeping world. Frizzled versions of several more breeds are recognized in the USA only. In the UK we have a breed called the Frizzle, which is virtually the same as US-standard Frizzled Plymouth Rocks, or in the case of (UK) Red Frizzles, (US) Frizzled Rhode Island Reds.

This mutation has been recorded in many, mostly warm, parts of the world from West Africa to the Pacific Islands; and as long ago as 1590, Pompilio Tagliaferro of Parma, Italy, had a flock of them that were mentioned by Ulisse Aldrovandi in his natural history book published in 1600.

Although quite rare in the UK, they are not officially a 'Rare Breed', because there is a breed club, The Frizzle Society of Great Britain. Most members keep the bantam version, which is available in a range of colour varieties. Plumage patterns never actually look right on Frizzles, although they have been attempted, therefore most breeders concentrate on self colours (Black, Blue, Buff, Lavender, Red and White) and white-tipped varieties (Black-Mottled and so on). The very few people who keep large Frizzles have concentrated on Whites so far. Creative poultry breeders might like to attempt to make large fowl versions of some of the other colours.

Blue, Black-mottle and Buff Frizzle bantam females. Only the White variety is seen in large Frizzles, so there is scope for creative fanciers to make large fowl versions of these three, and several more, attractive colours at present only existing in bantam form.

Frizzles are fairly easy to keep, although they need large houses as they must be kept inside when the weather is very cold or wet. Some bathing and preparation expertise is needed to show them successfully. Frizzling is caused by an incompletely dominant gene, which means that some normal, flat-feathered birds are produced each generation, as are some over-frizzled birds with weak and straggly plumage. Both of these, especially the flat-feathered ones, are very useful for breeding, even though they cannot be shown.

HAMBURGH (UK)/HAMBURG (USA) (LIGHT SOFT FEATHER/LARGE AND BANTAM)

This breed has a long, complex and fascinating history that spans several centuries and three countries, England, Germany and The Netherlands. The British name of the breed, Hamburgh (with the extra H at the end), was adopted about 1850 to include several almost identical breeds: Hamburgers from Germany, Hollandse Hoenders (and probably some Assendelftse Hoenders – still a separate recognized breed) from The Netherlands, and some now extinct local breeds from the north of England: Bolton Bays, Bolton Greys, Lancashire Moonies and Yorkshire Pheasants. Some strains of the last of these retained their separate identity and were revived as Old English Pheasant Fowl about 1914. These old breeds were bred for plumage markings, with breeders holding competitions in local pubs, long before the first 'proper' poultry show in 1845.

Hamburgh Bantams were first developed in the 1890s. Many of the UK strains are too big, leaving very little difference beween them and the large Hamburghs, which are one of the smaller Light Breeds. Fortunately, Dutch and German fanciers have been much more successful at breeding than smaller bantams and larger large 'Hollandse Hoenders' and 'Hamburgers'.

There are five traditional colour varieties: Black, Gold Pencilled, Silver Pencilled, Gold Spangled and Silver Spangled. American standards also include White Hamburgs, and Dutch and German fanciers have created several interesting new colour combinations of the Pencilled and Spangled patterns such as some with blue instead of the normal black markings.

Pencilled Hamburghs must be 'doubled mated' (*see* Glossary) because the male and female plumage patterns are so different. This would mean keeping two completely separate strains, one to produce exhibition quality males, the other to produce exhibition quality females, but very few keep both 'cock-breeders' and 'pullet-

Silver Spangled Hamburgh male. Only a few of each generation will have correct tail markings. Many either have poor spangles, or good spangles but with black shading in what should be the clear white part.

Gold Pencilled Hamburgh female. If a 'pullet-breeder' male is used, this beautiful colour variety is easier to breed than it looks, although the barring sometimes fails in tail feathers.

breeders'. Most just have one or the other. Many specialists also practise double mating with Blacks and Spangleds, but it's not essential with these varieties.

Hamburgh hens are good layers of white-shelled eggs, although their eggs are fairly small. The hens seldom go broody. They are an active breed that need generous outside runs with very high fences. Chicks should be handled and petted to tame them if they are to be entered in shows when fully grown.

HOUDAN (RARE BREED, LARGE AND BANTAM)

Houdan, their place of origin, is a town to the west of Paris. It is not known for sure when this breed was developed, but they were certainly well established by 1860. Houdans are a crested breed, and

Houdan female. This bird has very even distribution of its white spots. Many fail by having an almost completely white crest.

are considerably heavier than Polands and other European crested breeds. Their weight and the distinctive extra hind toe on each foot suggests that they were made by crossing crested chickens with Dorkings. The process from initial crossing to established new breed probably happened during the 1830s and 1840s. Houdans were exported to the UK and USA in 1865, and have continued to be bred in both countries in very limited numbers since then. A strain of Houdan Bantams was made about 1890. It is not known if the bantams bred now are related to these or are a modern remake.

In general build, Houdans are a practical, medium-weight chicken; so their ornamental features (crest, unusual 'leaf' comb, beard and extra hind toes) do not mean they are purely a show breed. The main colour variety is Black-Mottled, but White Houdans have also existed (but even rarer) since 1870.

Like all breeds with crest and beards, Houdans need a bit more care than 'normal' chickens, but they are not too demanding for reasonably enthusiastic beginners. As they are rare, there may not be any existing breeders near you from which to buy stock, but if there are, they are well worth considering.

INDIAN GAME (UK)/CORNISH (USA) (HARD FEATHER, LARGE AND BANTAM)

The different names for this breed in the UK and USA reflect its origins – it was made in Cornwall, but in great part from birds imported from India. During the eighteenth and early nineteenth centuries merchant ships on their way back to England from the Far East usually called in at Falmouth or Plymouth harbours before going on to their final destination. Sometimes the ship owners sent riders down (from London perhaps) with revised instructions. This was, of course, long before the invention of radio or any other means of communications. The seamen were allowed to earn a little extra by bringing Asil and other Asian fighting cocks back with them to sell to cockfighting enthusiasts in Cornwall and Devon. These birds were then often crossed with Old English Game, and these crosses eventually became a breed, 'Indian Game'.

Not all of the crosses were very good fighters, and anyway cock-fighting was banned in England in 1849 (although it continued in secret), and as 'Indian Game' were big, muscular birds, many of them were sold to normal farmers who crossed them with ordinary hens. The resulting crossbred cockerels were considerably larger and meatier than those they had bred before. The Indian Game Club was formed in 1886, followed by a showing standard in 1896. Specialist breeders, now concentrating on showing them, gradually selected for larger, broader bodies and shorter legs to suit the needs of their now significant secondary market. Top show birds could be sold for extraordinary prices, so they remained a priority, but 'the rest' were in steady demand from farmers as their reputation as a table bird sire spread from the south-west to the rest of Britain. Pure Indians were rather slow-growing, and Indian Game hens were always useless layers. Table bird producers crossed Indian Game cocks with heavy-breed hens such as Dorkings, Faverolles, Orpingtons or Sussex.

When they were exported to the USA, breeders there decided to change their name to Cornish to make it absolutely clear that they were now a meat breed, not a fighting breed. American breeders created a new colour variety, 'White Cornish', which went on to be incorporated into today's hybrid broilers. At first there had only been one colour of Indians/Cornish, the 'Dark', in which the males were mostly glossy black with some dark brown in neck and saddle hackles and the females a very attractive glossy brown and black double-laced pattern. British breeders then created Jubilee Indian Game, launched in 1897, the year of Queen Victoria's Diamond Jubilee to celebrate her sixtieth year on the throne. Jubilees are the same pattern as Darks, but with all black parts changed to (nearly) white. American breeders created White Laced Red Cornish, which are a single laced pattern, similar to Buff Laced Wyandottes. Several more colour varieties have been developed in the USA, but the only

Indian Game/Cornish bantams, breeding group. It is normal practice to cross Dark and Jubilee Indians in the UK and many other countries, but not possible with US Dark and White Laced Red Cornish.

other colour recognized in the UK and elsewhere is the Blue, which is also a variation of the Dark's pattern.

Several strains of Indian Game Bantams were made *circa* 1880–1914, and these followed the changes in the shape of large Indians during the twentieth century, gradually getting wider in the body and shorter in the leg. Many, probably most, Indian Game Bantams have been well over the official standard weights. It has proved difficult to produce an ideal combination of birds small enough to be a bantam while retaining the characteristic massive body shape, thick legs and so on. The old saying, 'Trying to fit a quart into a pint pot', sums up the conundrum of Indian Game Bantams, and their fascination to the many fanciers who have kept them all their lives.

Their short legs and massive body shape has led to fertility and hatching problems. Many fanciers use less extreme males for breeding to overcome these difficulties. Even Indian Game enthusiasts will admit they are probably not an ideal breed for beginners. Top-quality Indians are usually rather expensive, but longer-legged, less extreme-bodied birds are much cheaper.

IXWORTH (RARE BREED)

This breed was made by Reginald Appleyard, who also created the

White Ixworth male.

Silver Appleyard duck at his home in the Suffolk village of Ixworth. He started his Ixworth chicken-breeding programme in 1931, first showing his new breed in 1938. They were intended to be a meat breed, but progress was halted by the Second World War. Although the war ended in 1945, food and raw material shortages continued well into the 1950s, by which time the growth rates of American broiler hybrids were well in advance of the Ixworths and the other similar breeds produced in the UK in the same period. Ixworths were the only one to survive to the present day, and are now being used by some producers in the free-range/organic market. Mr Appleyard also made a bantam version of his Ixworth, but these probably died out by about 1960.

The main breeds used to make Ixworths were White Sussex and Jubilee Indian Game, which is obvious in their appearance. They have a pea comb and the general build of Jubilee Indians, with white plumage, skin, shanks and feet from White Sussex. Plumage quantity is half-way between the two. Ixworths are not bred outside the UK, the nearest equivalent breed in the USA and Canada being the Chantecler.

JAPANESE OR CHABO BANTAM (TRUE BANTAM)

Chabo, the international name for this breed, is derived from Chiyanpa, the old Japanese name for south-east Asia, the region that now includes Malaysia, Thailand and Vietnam. Roughly similar bantams exist in these countries today, and are almost certainly the basis of the Serama Bantam, which have been established in Malaysia since the 1990s. Chabos have a much longer continuously documented history. They were featured in Japanese paintings from about 1600, which indicates this was the time they were first imported to Japan. A Black-Tailed-Buff Chabo cock is also in 'The Poultry Yard', a painting by Dutch artist Jan Steen (*circa* 1660). It was almost certainly sent to Holland from the Dutch trading post on the island of Decima, virtually the only link between Japan and the rest of the world from 1636 until 1867, when successive Japanese emperors closed their country off to avoid disruption of its rigid social system by outside influences. As can be imagined, Chabo Bantams were very rare outside Japan until the 1870s. Since then there have been enough enthusiasts around the world to ensure there are classes of them at virtually every poultry show held. The breed clubs for them around the world have an enviable tradition of maintaining close international links.

Black-tailed Buff Japanese/Chabo male.

Black-tailed White Japanese/Chabo pair. Compare the tail markings of the BTB and BTW males. They should be identical, black with an even, thin edging (buff or white). Both birds won prizes at shows because no one else had any better. Some beginners fear their birds are not good enough to show. In some cases they may be right, but sometimes, despite breed faults, theirs are as good as everyone else's.

45

Grey Frizzled Japanese/Chabo male. There are also Silkie-feathered versions of this breed.

The main features of Japanese/Chabo Bantams are very short legs and a long tail that is carried very upright. There are many varieties within the breed, including frizzle and silkie forms, a variety with exceptionally large comb and wattles, and a black-skinned, black-plumaged variety. Among the many other plumage colours, two are particularly associated with Chabos: Black-Tailed-White and Black-Tailed-Buff. There are infertility and hatchability problems associated with their short legs, and this feature means they need specialized housing. Read one of the specialist books on them before buying.

JERSEY GIANT (RARE BREED IN THE UK, MORE POPULAR IN THE USA)

Black Jersey Giants have also been called Black's Jersey Giants and Jersey Black Giants because they were developed by brothers John

Blue Jersey Giant male. This colour variety is a relatively recent creation, probably made about 1970, although they are probably similar to the long extinct 'Jersey Blue', bred in the USA in the nineteenth century.

46

and Thomas Black of Jobstown, New Jersey *circa* 1890–1900 to provide extra large table birds for the hotels and restaurants of Boston, New York and Philadelphia. They made them from crosses of Brahmas, Langshans and the now very rare Java. Blue and White Jersey Giants were made later. Jersey Giant Bantams are standardized in the USA, but not in the UK.

Jersey Giants are fairly conventional in general shape, with smallish single combs and dark eyes. White Giants have greenish shanks and feet, and these parts are dark with yellow soles to the feet on Blacks and Blues. This was considered important when selecting breeding stock because American consumers traditionally preferred yellow-skinned table birds, and the soles of their feet are the only part of their skin clearly visible on a live bird.

As their name suggests, they are huge, with adult cocks weighing 6kg (13lb) and hens 4.5kg (10lb). They obviously need larger than normal houses, nest boxes and so on and a flock of them will get through a lot of chicken food. Like most of the other very large breeds, they are quiet, docile and do not need very high fencing to keep them in their runs. A really big Giant will impress most show judges, and will no doubt impress your friends, but a large flock of them (groups of all three colours perhaps) could become an expensive hobby.

KO-SHAMO (HARD FEATHER)

Although an ancient breed in Japan, Ko-Shamo have only become known to American and European fanciers since the 1980s. They are not, as many fanciers in the western world first assumed, simply a miniature version of large Shamo, but a related, much smaller breed; in the same way that Whippets are not miniature Greyhounds, although they appear to be so to the general public. Ko-Shamo have become very popular in the UK since the late 1990s, in part because they are wonderful little characters that can became very tame. Palaeontologists have discovered that birds are very closely related to dinosaurs, a relationship that is more obvious on Ko-Shamo than most other birds.

In Japan there are several other related breeds: Chibi-Shamo, Kinpa, Nankin-Shamo, Yakido and Yamato-Gunkei. Most of these have also been exported to Europe, but are too rare to be fully covered in this book intended for beginners.

Ko-Shamo have very scanty plumage, with bare red skin showing through along the breast bone, around the vent and on the 'elbow'

Black-red Ko-Shamo male. The line of bare red skin along the breast bone is an essential breed characteristic, as is the short neck-feathering that reveals broad shoulders.

joints of the wings. Associated with this scanty plumage is the tendency for most Ko-Shamo to be 'split-wing'. This gap between the primary and secondary wing feathers is a show disqualifying fault on all breeds except for Ko-Shamo and its relations, where it is almost mandatory. Their other key feature is their head character. Ko-Shamo have a very compact comb and no wattles. Instead they have wrinkled facial skin and a throat dewlap that gets more developed with age. Additional features to be considered are prominent eyebrow bones, a short, thick break and thick shanks with multiple lines of scales. Fine details of plumage colour and pattern do not matter on Ko-Shamo, however, the most prehistoric-looking bird wins, whatever colour it is.

KRAIENKÖPPE (GERMANY)/TWENTSE (NETHERLANDS) (RARE BREED, LARGE AND BANTAM)

This breed originated on both sides of the border between Germany and The Netherlands, and was given a different name in each country. About 1890, Malay cocks were bred with assorted farmyard hens, the resulting crossbreds later being mated with Silver Duck-wing Leghorns. They were established as a new breed during the 1920s, and work started on the creation of a bantam version in the 1930s. Both size versions were largely remade after the disruption of

Silver Kraienköppe/Twentse male.

Silver Kraienköppe/Twentse female.

49

the Second World War, although some of the earlier strains may have survived to contribute to them. They are attractive birds with a compact walnut comb and a large fanned tail. There are two colour varieties, Gold and Silver. Kraienköppes have been bred by a few fanciers in the UK since the 1970s.

LAKENVELDER (RARE BREED, LARGE AND BANTAM)

These, like the Kraienköppe/Twentse above, were also made on both sides of the Dutch/German border. In this case, the difference in naming is minor, being Lakenfelder (with an F) in Germany. Their main feature is their unusual plumage pattern: solid black neck and tail (plus some black wing markings) contrasting with white body and legs. There is also a breed of Lakenvelder cattle, with a similar black and white colour scheme, both named after the Dutch village of Lakervelt, south of Utrecht. The chicken breed was recorded there in 1727. The bantam version is a recent creation produced in the 1970s, and even newer is the blue and white variety.

Lakenvelders are similar to other active light breeds in terms of egg production and their need for outside runs with high fences. They are easy and economical to keep, but remain rare because only a modest proportion have the correct plumage pattern. Most birds have some black and white feathers growing in the wrong places. The careful removal of a few of these feathers can greatly improve their chances of winning at the shows. Be aware that their juvenile

Lakenvelder male. This bird has excellent solid black neck feathering, but some faulty black feathers on its breast. It is still better than most shown, so do not expect perfection with this breed. The judges are aware of the problems.

plumage is not exactly the same as their adult plumage, so they cannot be selected for pattern until fully mature.

LANGSHAN (US STANDARD), CROAD LANGSHAN (HEAVY SOFT FEATHER)
MODERN LANGSHAN (RARE BREED), GERMAN LANGSHAN (RARE BREED)
CHINESE LANGSHAN (AUSTRALIAN STANDARD)

Major F.T. Croad imported the first Langshans known to the western world in 1872 from northern China. They were large black fowls with slightly feathered legs and feet; fairly similar to the first importations of Black Shanghaes/Cochins except that Langshans had white skin, whereas the Shanghaes/Cochins had yellow skin. There was initially some argument about the relationship between the two breeds, which went on to lead to the development of the five standardized breeds named above from one importation. Read the Langshan chapter in *Rare Poultry Breeds* (David Scrivener, The Crowood Press) for the complete story.

There was no doubt some variation among the Langshans brought to the west from China in 1872 and the following years, and

Black Croad Langshan male.

51

ABOVE: Black Modern Langshan, young male. When fully mature, it would have been somewhat thicker set, but still significantly taller and tighter-feathered than a Croad.

LEFT: Blue German Langshan bantam male. Ideally, its tail should be higher, but the bird was probably stretching up to look at the photographer.

American Standard, Australian Standard and Croad Langshans are all (despite their minor differences) similar direct descendants of them. They are all fine big birds, yet still quite active, with slightly feathered feet. The main colour variety of all of them is still Black, but there are also Whites.

The Modern Langshan is by far the rarest of this group, with an estimated total world population of fewer than forty birds, all in England. There were displays of more than double the total world population today at some shows in the early twentieth century. Modern Langshans are taller than Croads, with tighter plumage, less leg and foot feather and a smaller, 'whipped' (that is, not fanned) tail.

German Langshans were developed in Germany and Austria by crossing Langshans imported from Major Croad with Plymouth Rocks and other Chinese imports. The new German Langshan was officially established when a breed club was formed in 1895. A bantam version was added by 1912. German Langshans do not have any shank or foot feathering. They are tall, elegant birds with a characteristic 'wine glass' body outline when viewed in profile.

Large German Lanshans briefly appeared at British shows during the 1980s, but there may not be any in the UK at the time of writing (2007). The bantam version is still classed as a Rare Breed in the UK, but it is getting much more popular. They would be an excellent breed for a beginner, both as potential show birds or simply as pretty and productive garden pets. There are three main colour varieties, Black, Blue and White; and several rarer colours: Barred, Red, Brown-red, Lemon-blue, Birchen, Silver-blue, Columbian and Buff-Columbian. Anyone thinking of starting with German Langshan Bantams should ask one of the breeders to explain the details of the desired body shape, tail carriage and so on, at a show where there are some on display to compare the good with the not so good.

LEGHORN (LIGHT SOFT FEATHER, LARGE AND BANTAM)

Leghorn is the Anglicized version of the Italian city and port of Livorno. Productive laying hens were sent from there to America, the first recorded shipment going to a Mr Ward of New York in 1835. There were many more shipments from then until about 1870, by which time American farmers had considerably improved them, both in terms of egg-laying performance and their appearance. At this time most were either 'Brown' (actually Black-red/Partridge pattern) or White, but the colour and markings of the Browns were very variable, and few of the Whites were really pure snow-white – but they were perfected by American breeders. Leghorns were sent to England from the USA, the first recorded shipment being in 1869. Meanwhile, the same original stock was being sent overland to farmers in Germany and Austria. As Livorno had no relevance for these imports, they named them Italieners.

Very large-scale commercial egg production was first developed in America, where the first very large incubators and other equipment to make it possible were also invented. As consumers in the major cities on the east and west coasts preferred white-shelled eggs, all the selective breeding programmes were based on White Leghorns, which are still (in modified form) the basis of all white egg-laying hybrids. By the 1920s poultry showing was becoming a separate activity from large-scale poultry farming, although the shows continued to be a 'shop window' for smaller-scale breeders who were breeding to supply domestic poultry keepers. During the 1920s and 1930s different 'Exhibition' and 'Utility' versions of some of the most important breeds were developed, and the Leghorn was

Exchequer Leghorn male. This unusual pattern should be maintained as a random mix of black and white. Do not breed from birds that tend towards Black-mottles (black feathers with white tips).

US-type Light Brown Leghorn bantam female. Leghorns in the USA and Canada have smaller combs, wattles and lobes, and larger tails, than Leghorns in the UK. There is a separate Dark Brown variety in the USA, not bred in the UK. UK Brown Leghorns are similar in colour, but not identical, to US Light Browns.

one of these breeds. To further complicate matters, the American Exhibition Leghorn was completely different from the British Exhibition Leghorn. Exhibition Leghorn/Italieners in The Netherlands, Germany and Austria were similar to each other, and not too different from the Utility strains that were much the same everywhere.

American Exhibition Leghorns have a relatively small comb, wattles and ear lobes and a very large fanned tail. British Exhibition Leghorns are the opposite: very large comb, wattles and ear lobes and a small 'whipped' tail. Utility/Dutch/German Leghorns/Italiener are halfway between these two in these parts. There are large and bantam versions of all of them.

There are many colour varieties of Leghorns, although not all of the colours are available in all of the types. The most typical, 'extreme' if you prefer, American and British types are seen in the two original colours: Brown (divided into Light Brown and Dark Brown in the USA) and White. Other colours include: Black, Blue, Blue-red, Crele (*see* Legbars in Autosexing Breeds), Cuckoo, Exchequer (a random mix of black and white), Gold Duckwing, Silver Duckwing and Pile. Most Leghorns have single combs, but rose combs are also permitted.

Leghorns are easy to keep as garden pets and layers. They are active birds that need high run fences to keep them in. The cocks are noisy and frequent crowers, so they may not be a popular choice with your neighbours in the suburbs. Leghorn hens seldom go broody at all, and the few that do give up long before the eggs hatch, so an incubator will be needed.

Considerable expertise is needed to successfully show White Leghorns of all types, so beginners should start with one of the other colours. The large single combs of British-type Leghorns (and to a lesser extent Utility, Dutch and German types) should be upright on males and flopping over on females. Most exhibitors concentrate on showing females, with the cockerels only being entered in a few shows just as they reach maturity. Their combs are usually upright for a few months, then they flop over, and the males are then just kept at home for breeding.

Black-red Malay male.

MALAY (HARD FEATHER, LARGE AND BANTAM)

Malays are very tall, with a very long neck and legs. This is accentuated by their sparse plumage with bare red skin showing along the breast bone, around the vent and on the 'elbow' joints of their wings. They have a compact walnut comb, prominent eyebrow bones and a very thick beak. All these features combine to give them a prehistoric, dinosaur-like appearance that usually provokes an instant love or hate reaction when people first see them.

Like Indian Game (*see above*), Exhibition Malays have a strong traditional link with Cornwall in south-west England. Malay Bantams were made by English fanciers in the 1880s, and were very popular until 1914. Since then, there have been more breeders of large and bantam Malays in Germany than the UK. Malay Bantams present a similar problem to breeders as do Indian Game Bantams – that is, how to preserve their characteristic height and powerful build on a bird small enough to be an acceptable bantam. Seek advice from experts before buying Malays.

MARANS (HEAVY SOFT FEATHER, LARGE AND BANTAM)

Famed for the dark brown eggs they lay, Marans are a favourite with smallholders and back garden poultry keepers, including many beginners. Marans have lightly feathered feet in France and unfeathered feet in Britain; the plumage colours are also different in the two countries. As these differences often puzzle poultry keepers, its history needs to be told in detail.

Marans is a town in western France, just north of La Rochelle. In the 1870s some Langshans, then the only dark brown breed available, were imported and crossed with farmyard chickens. The crossbreds were gradually refined into a new breed. Madame Rousseau, from L'Ile d'Elle, did a lot to stabilize the colour and size of both the birds and their eggs during the 1920s. Her improved strain, although still variable, impressed Lord Greenway and his poultry manager, Mr J.S. Parkin when they saw them at the 1929 Paris Poultry Show, and they had some sent over to his farm in Kent.

Marans had not yet been formally standardized in France, so it was not too unreasonable for Lord Greenway to favour the type he thought best. Some had feathered feet, others didn't, and as feathered footed birds are susceptible to scaly leg mite, clean legs were preferred. Of the several plumage colours among Lord Greenway's

Cuckoo Marans female, UK type.

Marans, Dark Cuckoo, Golden Cuckoo and Silver Cuckoo had the advantage that most day-old cockerel chicks were noticeably lighter than their sisters.

Meanwhile, back in France, Marans had to be standardized by the French National Poultry Club, and the clean-legged (that is, not feather-legged), Cuckoo-barred type favoured by Lord Greenway was too similar to a number of already standardized French, Belgian and Dutch breeds for them to recognize yet another one. Therefore, Marans in France were standardized with slightly feathered feet and the main colour varieties were Copper-black and Black-red/Wheaten. French-type Marans have also been bred in the UK since about 2000.

British-type Marans Bantams were created by Ken Bosley of Wantage, Berkshire. He first exhibited them at the 1953 National Show. French-type Marans Bantams are a much more recent creation, and none have been seen in the UK so far (2007).

Marans, British or French, large or bantam, are easy to keep and an excellent choice for beginners. Marans' eggs often win top awards in the egg section of poultry shows, although the birds seldom (if ever) go on to win 'Best in Show' or other major awards.

Dark-brown eggshells are their most important breed characteristic, but this can sometimes be at the expense of egg numbers. There seems to be a limit to the amount of brown pigment they can produce, so there is less for each egg from the best layers. Related to this is the fact that the first eggs they lay in the early spring will be darker than those laid by the same bird a few months later. Make allowances for this when deciding which eggs to incubate, and try to keep track of which hen is laying which egg and how many of them. This is not too difficult if you only keep a few hens. Take care when buying stock as there is a very similar, part Marans-based, commercial hybrid called the 'Speckledy'. They do lay brown eggs, but not brown enough, and some people have crossed proper Marans with Speckledies – with inevitable mix-ups.

MARSH DAISY (RARE BREED, LARGE ONLY)

Marsh Daisies were a briefly popular breed with British smallholders in the 1920s and 1930s which, by chance, have survived through to the present day. Their story started at Marshside (hence their name), Lancashire, about 1880, where John Wright kept a mixture of crossbreed chickens. Charles Moore of Doncaster bought some of them in 1913, did some more crossing and promoted the result as a new breed after the 1914–18 war. More people started to keep them, and a Marsh Daisy Club was formed. Present-day Marsh Daisies are descended from two important flocks in the 1930s at Watchet and Willington in Somerset.

They are an attractive and practical breed with a rose comb and greenish coloured shanks and feet. Five colour varieties are standardized: Black, Brown, Buff, Wheaten and White. Blacks and Whites are both probably extinct. The other three varieties seem to have been crossed, so most of the few remaining Marsh Daisies are

Marsh Daisy male.

*Black Minorca
bantam female. This
is the exhibition-type
bred in the UK and
the rest of Europe.
US-bred Minorcas
have fanned tails and
smaller lobes.*

of indeterminate colour. If stock can be located it would make an excellent project for an enthusiastic beginner to help recreate all three colours as they were originally bred in the 1920s.

MINORCA (LIGHT SOFT FEATHER, LARGE AND BANTAM)

The ancestors of standard-bred Minorcas may have come from the Spanish island of Menorca, but the breed as it has been known for well over a century was made in England. Minorcas have larger combs and white ear lobes, and are larger birds generally than were their ancestors on Menorca. They are the largest of the Light Breeds, with weights equal to the smallest of the Heavy Breeds. The change from ancestral type to the larger exhibition type started in south-west England in the early nineteenth century, with later changes by breeders in the north of England. Minorca Bantams were first made about 1890–1900, but were rare until the 1930s. Minorcas in the USA have much smaller ear lobes than those bred everywhere else.

Both sizes of Minorcas are good layers of white eggs, although they were not used by large-scale egg producers as much as Leghorns, probably because being bigger birds they ate more chicken food. They were a very popular show breed before 1940, and surplus pullets were certainly sold in large numbers to back garden poultry keepers. At the shows, most attention was given to their headpoints: comb, wattles, dark eye colour and white ear lobes.

Despite the wording in British Poultry Standards, breeders and judges have strived for the largest possible lobes, while retaining a smooth surface, a good shape and avoiding any white spreading from the lobe to the face, which should still be red. Black has always been the most popular plumage colour. Blues and Whites are also standardized in most countries, plus Buff in the USA. Some expertise is needed to produce really good show birds, but they regularly win top awards.

MODERN GAME (HARD FEATHER, LARGE AND BANTAM)

This is a very unusual tall and slender breed, its long legs being accentuated by tight plumage. Large Modern Game are quite rare, but are not in the Rare Breed section because there is a Modern Game Club, most of the members of which keep Modern bantams.

Modern Game were developed in the decades following 1849, when cockfighting was banned in the UK and breeders turned to showing. Over the years new breeders and judges became involved who had never even seen a cockfight, and they preferred taller, tighter-feathered birds.

The breed changed gradually, an intermediate form (about 1870– 80) being called 'Exhibition Game'. Not everyone approved of these changes, so in the 1880s some breeders revived the older strains (that had been bred by a lot of people who had continued cockfighting in secret) under a new name, Old English Game (*see below*). Once this group had gone their separate way, the new generation continued to make their show birds even taller and tighter-feathered, resulting in Modern Game as we know them today, during the 1890s. Large Moderns were a very popular show breed for the few years up to 1914, with some birds being sold for £100 or more, a fortune in those days. The hard times of two world wars and the economic depression between them ended this, so large Modern Game have been a rarity ever since.

Modern Game Bantams are elegant, tame and tiny little things that could be kept in the smallest of gardens. They did not each much, so they continued to thrive through these difficult decades. Incomes and living standards are much higher now, but space is even more limited than it was then, so Modern Game Bantams have continued to be a favourite with poultry show exhibitors. They make excellent pets because they are instinctively very tame and friendly with people and are too small and dainty to do any damage

Partridge Modern Game bantam female.

to lawns or flower beds. As might be expected, they are not a practical laying breed.

There are a lot of colour varieties to choose from: Black-red/Partridge, Black-red/Wheaten, Gold Duckwing, Silver Duckwing, Blue-red, Pile, Birchen, Brown-red, Lemon-blue, Silver-blue, Black, Blue and White.

Modern Game males have traditionally been 'dubbed', that is, the surgical removal of the comb, wattles and ear lobes. This has been banned in some countries, and may be banned in more. However, a Modern with a full set of headgear simply doesn't look 'right', their snaky, elegant style is lost. Breeders in Germany and The Netherlands have been experimenting with crosses to obtain Moderns with small pea or walnut combs to preserve the desired style within the law. At the time of writing (2007) it was too early to say how these matters would be resolved.

NANKIN (RARE BREED, A TRUE BANTAM)

These buff-coloured bantams were very common two centuries ago, which was probably the cause of their downfall. When poultry

Nankin male. More selective breeding is required to reduce size and improve breed type and style to recreate Nankins as they were in the nineteenth century.

shows started in the mid-nineteenth century they were regarded as just country bantams, not really appreciated as a proper breed. However, they were used to make buff, red and gold varieties of other breeds, including Gold Sebrights. It was feared that Nankins had become extinct, possibly before the First World War, but a strain had been kept going by the Martin family of Wisbech, Cambridge-shire, and in 1955 they were assisted by Mrs Peters of Ringmer, Sussex. Additional Rare Poultry Society members have taken up Nankins since the 1970s, but they remain rare and are much bigger and less stylish than the descriptions (and one known photograph) in the old poultry books indicate they were.

Nankins should be small and jaunty, with a large, well-fanned tail. The only known old photo (in *The Encylopedia of Poultry*, J.S. Hicks, *circa* 1921) of Nankins shows birds that seem to have been very simi-lar in size and shape to today's US-type Old English Game Bantams. The buff plumage of Nankins is not as even in all parts as other buff breeds, and the tail feathers are partly black or bronzy. Both single and rose combs, and either white or blue shanks and feet, have been recognized throughout their history. They have no connection at all with the Nankin-Shamo mentioned in the Ko-Shamo section.

NEW HAMPSHIRE RED (HEAVY SOFT FEATHER, LARGE AND BANTAM)

Professor A.W. 'Red' Richardson, Head of the Animal Husbandry Department of the University of New Hampshire, developed New

New Hampshire Red male.

Hampshire Reds from selected strains of Rhode Island Reds between 1910 and 1935. New Hampshires are a lighter colour than Rhodes and have better table-bird conformation. Commercially, they have been used by hybrid breeding companies, and as pure breeds have been particularly popular in Germany and The Netherlands, where the bantam version was created. They have only been kept by hobbyists in the UK in significant numbers since the 1980s, where they seem to be attracting a lot of interest from beginners to our hobby, and rightly so.

Although they are a relatively new pure breed (1935, compared to other breeds that have existed for centuries) they represent many peoples' idea of what a traditional chicken should be. They are very productive, and the hens will go broody and hatch their own eggs. Most of their plumage is in shades of bright golden-brown, with a black tail, wing markings and a little neck striping. There is an attractive new blue-tailed version in The Netherlands that will probably be bred in the UK soon. New Hampshires are an excellent breed for beginners to our hobby.

NORFOLK GREY (RARE BREED)

As would be imagined from their name, this rare breed was made in the English county of Norfolk, which is where most flocks are still to be found. There have never been any Norfolk Grey Bantams and they have never been exported. The Birchen Niederrheiner is an almost identical German breed, but they are not connected.

Norfolk Grey female.

They were made by Mr Fred Myhill of Norwich, who first exhibited them at the 1920 London Dairy Show under the name 'Black Marias' – the name was changed to Norfolk Grey in 1925. There was a Norfolk Grey Club, with quite a few people keeping them, until the Second World War, when they seemed to disappear. They were next seen at poultry shows about 1970, after a flock of the old strain was said to have been discovered, which was revived with a few crosses with the breeds that were known to have been used to make them originally.

Norfolk Greys are an attractive medium/heavy breed with mostly black plumage except for the neck and (on males) saddle hackles, which are silvery white with black centre striping. They are easy to keep and would be a good choice if you can locate stock for sale.

NORTH HOLLAND BLUE (RARE BREED)

These are actually cuckoo-barred, not blue, but were said to appear blue when seen at a distance. They were developed in the early twentieth century in the Noord-Holland region of The Netherlands to supply table chickens to the Amsterdam markets. The clean leg/feather leg difference described in Marans also happened, in reverse, with North Hollands – they are clean-legged in The Netherlands and feather-legged in the UK. North Hollands were imported to the UK in 1934, with most of the breeders being table-bird producers in the counties around London. When they were effectively made redundant commercially by hybrid broilers, the UK type,

Norfolk Holland Blue female, UK-type.

feather-legged North Holland blue was only conserved to the present day because of the enthusiasm of one man – Les Miles, and he only had a suburban garden at Enfield, on the northern outskirts of London to keep them in. Les was an inspiring example of how one person with very limited facilities really can make a difference to the conservation of old breeds of poultry.

North Holland Blues are similar to Cuckoo Marans in general shape, size and colour except for their lightly feathered legs and slightly brighter and clearer plumage colour and barring. They are easy to keep and the cockerel chicks are lighter in colour than their sisters, which is helpful if you know that you will not need all the cockerels that hatch.

OLD ENGLISH GAME (HARD FEATHER, LARGE AND BANTAM)

This is a very popular and very complex breed as there are several distinct types: UK Carlisle-type, UK Oxford-type and US-type. OEG (the usual abbreviation used) in the USA are similar to UK Oxford-type, although not quite identical. Carlisle-type OEG are very different, being heavier, broader-bodied, with a higher wing carriage and a much smaller, tightly folded ('whipped') tail. The difference is even more pronounced when you compare OEG Bantams in the USA with OEG Bantams in the UK – only their name is the same! Specialist books should be consulted for a full explanation of how and why all these different types were developed.

Blue-red Carlisle type Old English Game pair. This front view of a Carlisle-type cock shows their body width.

Ginger Oxford type Old English Game pair. This colour variety is only seen on Oxfords, there are no Ginger Carlisles.

Spangled Old English Game bantam trio, Carlisle, UK-type. These are mainly judged on body shape, and these were winning birds despite their uneven spangling.

Blue Old English Game bantam male, US-type. OEG in the USA are similar to Oxford-type OEG in the UK. American breeders pay far more attention to details of plumage colour and markings than British OEG breeders (Carlisle or Oxford).

Lemon Blue Old English Game bantam female, US-type.

All types of OEG are available in a wide range of colour varieties, although not every colour exists in every type. American breeders place more emphasis on the colour and pattern being correct when judging at the shows, with British breeders and judges concentrating almost entirely on body shape and other physical features. The details are too complex to fully describe in a general book like this. A beginner is unlikely to perceive the difference between the 'Best of Breed' and an 'also ran' at a show, so anyone interested in keeping OEG will need experienced breeders to explain everything. There are also Muffed (bearded), Tasselled (with a small feathered crest) and Henny (hen-feathered males) OEG, all relatively rare sub-varieties usually seen among large Oxfords. OEG in general remain a very popular breed, but as there are many complexities to be understood, they may not be ideal for typical beginners.

OLD ENGLISH PHEASANT FOWL (RARE BREED)

Old English Pheasant Fowl and Derbyshire Redcaps are the only two of the ancient north of England poultry breeds that were not fully absorbed into the Hamburgh breed *circa* 1850–80. A group of enthusiasts tracked down the surviving farmyard flocks of what had previously been called Yorkshire Pheasant Fowl, and formed the Old English Pheasant Fowl Club in 1914. OEPF are still a light breed, but are larger, meatier and lay larger eggs than large Hamburghs (which had been selected for ideal show plumage pattern 1850–1914). Although the OEPF Club members stressed their usefulness as a

Old English Pheasant Fowl male.

Old English Pheasant Fowl female.

hardy farmers' breed, they did enter a fine lot between them at their annual club shows from the 1920s until the 1950s. OEPF have been very rare since then, there were never any OEPF Bantams and they are not bred outside the UK.

If you are able to locate any stock for sale, and have large grassy runs to go with your poultry houses, OEPF are a really beautiful, productive, hardy and historic breed that need a few more competent hobbyists to breed them. Because they are very similar to Derbyshire Redcaps it is not a good idea to keep both breeds – any accidental crossbreds produced by a bird flying over a run fence might not be identified as such, and so could mess up a strain if bred from.

ORLOFF (RARE BREED, LARGE AND BANTAM)

Although frequently called 'Russian Orloffs', this breed originally came from the Gilan province of northern Iran, then some were taken to Russia by Count Orloff (or Orlov). Poultry experts from Austria, Germany, the UK and USA saw Orloff Fowls at a large poultry show in 1899 at St Petersburg, resulting in them being exported to those countries in the following years. There was an Orloff club in the UK, 1915–39. Most of its members lived in Scotland and the north of England as it was generally agreed that Orloffs were not the best layers or fastest growing table breed, but they were able to thrive and were fair producers on cold hill farms where the main commercial breeds usually sickened and died. Orloffs were mainly bred as show birds in Germany, which is where Orloff Bantams were made in the 1920s.

69

Spangled Orloff male.

Orloffs are quite tall, muscular-looking birds. Their main breed characteristics are their headpoints: a small walnut or 'raspberry' comb, prominent eyebrow bones, a thick beak and a well-developed beard. The three main colour varieties are Mahogany, Spangled and White, with Blacks and Cuckoos having existed in the past. Orloff Bantams, especially the Spangled variety, are very pretty and deserve to be a lot more popular than they are. As large Orloffs are quite big birds they need appropriately large houses and runs, but apart from that, both sizes of Orloffs are easy to keep and worth considering if you are able to locate any stock for sale.

ORPINGTON (HEAVY SOFT FEATHER, LARGE AND BANTAM)

Both the Orpington chicken and Orpington duck breeds were created by William Cook and his son and daughter. William Cook was born at St Neots, Huntingdonshire, but moved to St Mary Cray, a village near Orpington in Kent, in 1869, where he started a business breeding poultry and selling a complete range of poultry keeping equipment, houses, books, and so on. His first new breed, the Black Orpington, was more like today's Australorps, and was made by crossing several breeds, the most important being Black Langshans. Orpingtons have been a much larger, fluffier breed for most of their history, this type being developed by Joseph

Partington of Lytham, Lancashire about 1890, only four years after Cook first launched his original type. Despite Cook's protests (his birds were much better layers than Partington's) most show judges started to give the top prizes (and the very generous prize money offered then) to the impressive-looking Partington type.

The Cook family created several more colour varieties of Orpingtons: White (1889), Buff (1894), Jubilee (1897 – not the same colour as Jubilee Indian Game, but also launched in Queen Victoria's Diamond Jubilee year), Spangled (1899), Blue and Cuckoo (both 1907). The Cooks were forced to follow the general trend and, for their show strains at least, keep the large 'feather duster' type. Buff Orpington Bantams were first made in the 1890s, but were not very good until well into the twentieth century. This is another of the breeds that tend to lose the massive appearance of the large breed they are supposed to represent in miniature when reduced to bantam size. Orpington Bantams are now available in all colour varieties.

Orpingtons of both sizes have won many major awards at the shows over the years and are also a popular garden pet breed, most people choosing Buffs. Large Orpingtons are very large indeed, and their housing must be designed to accommodate their needs – including extra-large nest boxes for the hens to lay in. Sunlight causes the colour of Buffs to fade and makes Blues and Whites go 'brassy', an unattractive yellowish tinge. This can be minimized if their outside runs have some trees growing in them for shade. Orpingtons are docile birds, so make excellent pets, even when the chickens seem to be bigger than the children keeping them! It would probably be more practical for beginners to choose the bantam version.

Buff Orpington pair.

PEKIN BANTAM (TRUE BANTAM IN THE UK)/COCHIN BANTAM (IN OTHER COUNTRIES)

As indicated by the alternative breed names, there have been difference of opinion about whether these bantams are, or are not, miniatures of large Cochins. Pekin Bantams in the UK are definitely lower to the ground and broader in proportion than large Cochins. Cochin Bantams, as standardized in most other countries, stand a little more upright, but not really upright enough to look like miniature Cochins even though they are classed as such. The low posture required in the UK is called the 'Pekin tilt', with the tip of the tail being higher than the head when they are standing normally and are happy and relaxed.

They were first 'discovered' by British and French soldiers when they were looting the Emperor of China's Palace in Peking/Beijing during the Opium Wars in 1860. Find a good history book for details of this shameful episode in our colonial history. A British officer sent some Buff Pekin Bantams from the palace gardens back to his friend, Mr Kerrick, in England. Black, White, Cuckoo and Partridge Pekins were sent back to England during the 1870s and 1880s, one hopes (unlike the first Buffs) after paying a fair price to their original owners.

These early imports had less foot feathering, were more upright in posture and their colours and (on Cuckoo and Partridge) markings were not as good or uniform as show exhibitors liked, so they began many decades of selective breeding to produce eventually the perfect little birds with their amazing foot feathering we see today. Several more colour varieties have been made since then, including Black-Mottled, Blue, Blue-Mottled, Columbian and Lavender.

Black Pekin pair.

As Pekins have extravagant foot feathering and a very profuse body plumage, which touches the ground, they are definitely not suitable for free ranging in a muddy farmyard. If it is intended to show them, they need the highest level of care and housing designed to keep them clean inside for most of the time, with access to your garden lawn on nice days. Those who just want Pekins as pets should still adopt at least some of the methods used by show exhibitors. If you have strong opinions about chickens being allowed outside to live in a 'natural' way – don't keep Pekins! It is very important for people to choose a breed that suits the environment they have available for their birds, as well as a breed that they happen to like.

PLYMOUTH ROCK (HEAVY SOFT FEATHER, LARGE AND BANTAM)

'The Plymouth Rock' is a granite boulder on the shore of Plymouth Bay, Massachusetts, the place where the Pilgrim Fathers landed in America in 1620 (apologies to readers in the USA for stating the obvious, but readers in the UK and elsewhere may not know that). The first breed of chicken given this iconic (to Americans) name was made by Dr John Bennett, who lived in nearby Plymouth City in 1847, but his breed died out and is not related to the second breed with the same name that we have today. Barred Plymouth Rocks were made by a group of breeders in Massachusetts and Connecticut in 1856–76, with Buff and White Plymouth Rocks being added to the range in the 1890s. Black Plymouth Rocks appeared, without anyone deliberately making them, among groups of Barred Rock chicks. They often simply called 'Rocks' in normal conversation among poultry keepers. Beginners must be aware that the commercial hybrid layers called 'Black Rocks' are not the same as standard Black Plymouth Rocks as recognized for showing. Commercials have some brown feathering mixed in with the black and usually have dark-coloured shanks and feet. An exhibition Black Rock must have completely black (with a green gloss) plumage and bright yellow shanks and feet.

There are now also Blue, Columbian, Partridge and Silver Pencilled Rocks, plus bantams in all colours. Large White Plymouth Rocks were widely used in the development of hybrid broilers, where selected strains of hens were crossed with selected strains of White Cornish cocks.

Barred Plymouth Rocks were first imported to the UK in 1872,

Barred Plymouth Rock female.

Black Plymouth Rock female. Note solid black, with a bright green gloss, plumage and bright yellow shanks and feet. Commercial 'Black Rock' layers have black and brown plumage and dark shanks. They should not be entered in shows, and are in fact a hybrid produced by a sex-linked crossing of commercial strains of Rhode Island Reds and Barred Rocks. Exhibition Black Plymouth Rocks, like this one, are quite rare.

when the breed was still in its early stages of development, by J.W. Ludlow, the specialist poultry, pigeon and cage bird artist. As happened with several other breeds, British fanciers concentrated so much on improving the showing aspects, in this case the barred plumage markings, that Plymouth Rocks lost many of their utility qualities. Show-winning Barred Rocks may have had very fine and sharp barring, but many of them were tall and skinny, no longer a useful table breed, by 1900. There was no large-scale poultry production in the UK then, and all the leading breeders were concentrating on the then considerable financial rewards from the show scene. American show exhibitors also greatly improved their strains, but they did not lose sight of the breed's original purpose. During the

1920s and 1930s separate exhibition and utility types were developed. In Germany this eventually resulted in their utility type being recognized for showing as a different breed – the Amrock.

The result of this breed history today is:

- Large and bantam Plymouth Rocks are still a popular breed in the USA.
- Large Plymouth Rocks are almost extinct in the UK; the bantams are moderately popular. (They are not classed as 'Rare' because there is a Plymouth Rock Club.)
- Plymouth Rocks and Amrocks in both sizes are still bred in Germany in moderate numbers.

Most of the few large Rocks bred in the UK are from imported strains, so are not quite as tall as the old show strains that effectively ruined the breed here. There are a few enthusiastic young fanciers trying to revive them here, and very smart their birds are too. Plymouth Rocks are a conventional looking breed, although there are a lot of details to get right on a show winner. All varieties need large houses and shaded (by trees perhaps) outside runs to keep looking at their best. Rocks must have rich yellow shanks and feet, which is why they need access to grass, but sunlight fades the colour of Buffs and makes Whites go brassy. It is a lot easier to provide this combination to bantams by using covered top movable arks, which is one reason why Plymouth Rock bantams remain more popular then the large fowl. Barred, Buff and White Rock Bantams remain more popular than the large fowl. Barred, Buff and White Rock Bantams should be fairly easy to locate and buy, but beginners intending to enter shows may have more success if they track down one of the rarer colour varieties.

POLAND (LIGHT SOFT FEATHER, LARGE AND BANTAM)

These crested chickens have been called Polands or Polish in England and America since the early nineteenth century, perhaps longer, but they have no connection to the country of Poland. The name is probably derived either from 'polled' (hornless cattle, which gave a dome-shaped head) or 'pollarded' (trees that have grown back into a lollipop shape after the branches have been cut off. Willows were once regularly cut back in this way to produce new shoots for basket making). The rounded shape of a Poland's crest is similar in shape. In Germany and The Netherlands they are divided into two breeds: Non-bearded, White Crested Blacks, White Crested Blues, Black Crested White and so on, are Hollandse Kuifhoenders; and Bearded, Laced and self-coloured varieties are Paduaners (Germany) or Nederlandse Baardkuifhoenders (The Netherlands). Padua/Padova is a city in northern Italy. Crested chickens like them have been bred in many parts of Europe, possibly including Poland, since the sixteenth century, but they seen to have been bred in greater numbers and the finest quality in The Netherlands. Bantam Polands were made independently in The Netherlands and the UK, where they were another of W.F. Entwisle's miniature creations. Frizzled versions of all colour varieties in both size versions are also recognized.

Gold Laced Poland female.

White Crested Blue Poland female.

Polands needs a lot of specialized care, housing and equipment if they are to be kept clean and in good condition. It should be obvious that this is the case for fanciers intending to show them, but much of the special care is just as necessary if they are only to be kept as pets at home. They are prone to mite infestation in their crests, so every bird must be regularly checked, and treated if necessary. Special water containers are essential to prevent them soaking their crest and beard every time they drink, which could eventually lead to colds and infections. A flock of Polands will lay enough eggs for the average family, although they have never been used for commercial egg production.

They are clearly not a suitable breed for most beginners to poultry keeping, although anyone who has previously kept another demanding pet, a long-haired cat or dog perhaps, is likely to be a quick learner. Visit an expert breeder before buying.

REDCAP (LIGHT SOFT FEATHER, LARGE AND BANTAM)

Mr W.H. Baker, a leading Redcap breeder in the 1920s and 1930s, said that half the Redcap breeders in the world lived within 10 miles of Bakewell (Derbyshire, England), which is why this breed is often called the Derbyshire Redcap. They have been spread out a little since then, but are unlikely to be available outside the UK. There is a Derbyshire Redcap Club in the UK, which is why they are not in the Rare Breed section here, despite being very rare indeed on a world-wide basis. Most Redcap Club members keep the large version,

Derbyshire Redcap male.

77

Derbyshire Redcap female.

although a few Redcap Bantams are seen at shows in Derbyshire and neighbouring counties.

Redcaps are related to, and similar to, Gold Spangled Hamburghs and Old English Pheasant Fowl. All three breeds are athletic enough to fly over normal hen-run fences, and any resulting accidental cross-bred chicks might be difficult to identify; so only keep one of the breeds. If you are able to provide large outside runs, essential for this traditional countryside breed, Redcaps are ideal for conservation-minded beginners. Their plumage, glossy black and brown, looks wonderful when a flock of them are running outside in the sunshine, which may not be apparent when you see them in a show hall.

RHODE ISLAND RED (HEAVY SOFT FEATHER, LARGE AND BANTAM)

Everyone has heard of these, even if they cannot name any other chicken breed, and they probably assume they are one of the really old breeds. In fact they were not recognized as an official breed by the American Poultry Association until 1904, which is relatively recent compared to many of the other breeds in this book. Their history can be traced back some fifty years before then, but the name 'Rhode Island Red' was not coined until 1892, when they were still at the 'prototype' stage. Rhodes then rapidly became one of the most commercially important breeds in the world, and was later used to make some hybrids. This is one of the few pure breeds where there are still different exhibition and utility types. It would be a mistake to say that one is 'better' or 'worse' than the other – it is simply a

Rhode Island Red female.

matter of anyone intending to keep Rhodes to have a clear idea which type would suit their needs.

Exhibition type RIRs are larger than the utility type and a darker, glossier colour. Most Rhodes have a smallish single comb, but there is also a rarer rosecombed variety. Rhode Island Whites are also standardized in America and a few other countries. RIR Bantams were first made in the 1920s, independently in several countries.

Rhodes are generally considered to be a good breed for beginners, although they are not as simple to breed for showing as they appear. Some show strains have rather poor feather quality, often having tatty tail feathers for no apparent reason. Two aspects that beginners often fail to notice are considered very important by Rhode specialists: eye colour should be red (it is often too light, almost yellow) and the deep red plumage colour should extend right down to the skin (the fluffy part near the skin is sometimes white or greyish, both faults).

ROSECOMB BANTAM (TRUE BANTAM)

Their ancestors probably came from south-east Asia, although some Victorian poultry books called them 'Black African Bantams'; but this was a very long time ago as Black Rosecomb Bantams are known to have been bred in England as far back as the late fifteenth century. Rosecombs have always been a pet breed, they are too small to be a practical chicken. When organized poultry shows started in the mid-nineteenth century, this was one of the breeds favoured by competitive exhibitors who used all their expertise to produce birds that were perfect down to the most minute detail. The breed name,

Rosecomb, is written as one word; they do, of course, have a rose comb, written as two words. In Germany the breed name is Bantam, their general word for miniature chickens being Zwerg (dwarf), and in The Netherlands they are called Javas.

Black Rosecombs have always been the most popular colour variety as black plumage gives the most striking contrast to their large white ear lobes and red comb, wattles and facial skin. Whites were the other historic variety, with Blues being added to the range in the 1920s and 1930s. Three separate strains of Blues were made by Dr G. Irwin Royce in California, Mr Ostermann in The Netherlands and Herbert Whitley in Devon. Mr Whitley had a large collection of blue varieties of many poultry breeds, plus blue rabbits and other animals. Many more colours have been developed in The Netherlands and Germany: Barred, Birchen, Black-Mottle, Black-red/Partridge, Black-red/Wheaten, Brown-red, Buff, Buff Columbian, Buff-Mottle, Columbian, Millefleurs and Silver Duckwing. There may be more.

Blacks, Blues and Whites usually have larger white ear lobes than the other colours, especially in the UK. They are also more likely to win 'Best of Breed' awards than the other colours, although the large lobes are often difficult to keep in good condition – they have a tendency to droop out of shape, have nasty brown scabs, and the white spreads to the rest of the face on older birds. Specialist exhibitors have to continually breed new birds to show, although the 'retired' show birds will live and lay as long as any other breed. Beginners to showing, and those who do not intend to show at all, will probably be happier with one of the pretty Dutch and German

Black Rosecomb female.

colour varieties that are now also available in limited numbers in the UK. Their smaller lobes are much less trouble and they are less prone to white in the face.

RUMPLESS GAME (RARE BREED, HARD FEATHER)

There are several rumpless (completely lacking a tail) breeds around the world, some of which are known to have existed for several centuries. Most of them are rumpless versions of local breeds such as the Barbu du Grubbe and Barbu d'Everberg already described. Rumpless Game are a rumpless version of Old English Game Bantams. Large Rumpless Game and Rumpless Modern Game Bantams also exist, but are very rare. This breed is associated with the Isle of Man, also the home of the tailless Manx Cat. Both the cats and the chickens were bred in much greater numbers than previously when the island's tourist industry developed in Victorian times. Customers at the many 'Farmhouse Cream Teas' businesses expected to see a few Rumpless Bantams and Manx Cats wandering around the garden, so the owners bought both, even if they had never kept these supposedly traditional Manx animals before.

Rumpless Game Bantams, often just called 'Rumpies', are now bred by several fanciers in all parts of the UK, but are still fairly rare. They often win 'Best Rare Breed' awards at the shows because non-specialist Rare Breed judges know they should be assessed exactly as the popular OEG Bantams, in all OEG colours, except for the tail.

Brown-red Rumpless Game bantam male.

Partridge Rumpless Game bantam female.

SCOTS DUMPY (LIGHT SOFT FEATHER, LARGE AND BANTAM)

Scots Dumpies are one of a few short-legged breeds around the world, and are very similar to Courtes Pattes (France), Krüper (Germany) and Luttehøne (Denmark). It is believed they have all existed for many centuries, but because they were simply smallholders' chickens very few details were documented before the mid-nineteenth century. A group of fanciers in Scotland started to create a strain of Scots Dumpy Bantams about 1912, that by the 1920s were often winning 'Best of Breed' awards over the original large Dumpies.

Their obvious main feature, very short legs, is accentuated by their body shape, which is not only deep and broad but also long. They also have a large tail that should not be carried too high. All these features combine to give an overall long and low appearance that has been called 'boat-shaped'. Dumpies have a smallish single comb, red ear lobes and their shanks and feet are white on lighter coloured varieties, black or slate on the Black variety. They were bred in a wide range of colour varieties in Scotland, but most show exhibitors have concentrated on (in order of popularity) Cuckoos, Blacks and Whites. Although Scots Dumpy enthusiasts stress that shape and size are more important than colour, and the historical correctness of the other colour varieties (for example, Gold or Silver hackled Blacks), the three more conventional varieties are likely to win more awards at most local poultry shows with non-specialist judges.

Cuckoo Scots Dumpy pair.

Dumpy hens are good layers, broodies and gentle mothers. Surplus cockerels are meaty and of good conformation. They are faily docile birds, so would be a good choice for beginners. Design their houses with their limited mobility in mind, they cannot manage high steps. The best (for showing) short-legged cockerels are likely to have trouble mating, and the gene responsible for their short legs causes some of the embryos to die during incubation. Some Dumpies will be hatched each year with longer legs, so the normal procedure is to breed from longer-legged Dumpy cockerels and short-legged hens. The longer-legged hens will be useful layers and broodies, but do not breed from them as a flock of all long-legged Dumpies is rather a contradiction in terms – they would effectively cease to be Scots Dumpies at all. Any good specimens you breed will be showable for several years, especially large Dumpies, which are seldom quite large enough until two years old.

SCOTS GREY (LIGHT SOFT FEATHER, LARGE AND BANTAM)

This is Scotland's other surviving traditional poultry breed; the third, 'Dunbartonshire Fowl', died out during the nineteenth century. As with Dumpies, Scots Greys are known to have existed for centuries, but very little detail was documented before the

Scots Grey bantam pair.

'Scotch Grey Club' was formed in 1885. The name was changed to Scots Grey Club in 1923. Show exhibitors changed the breed during this period (1885–1923). Before then, Scots Greys were larger birds with fairly coarse cuckoo barring – probably very similar to (and related to) Coucou de Rennes, a rare breed from northern France. The showmen concentrated on refining the plumage markings into sharp and precise barring, and went for slim, elegant, light-breed body shape. Many old poultry books refer to 'Cuckoo Bantams' as being an ancient variety that were roughly similar to miniature Scots Greys. The bantam breeders were ahead of their large-fowl-keeping friends in the selective breeding process, with a Mr Mitchell of Paisley being the first recorded exhibitor of Scots Grey Bantams in 1866. Scots Greys of both sizes are very rare, if bred at all, outside the UK, but are not officially 'Rare' here because the Scots Grey Club is still supporting them.

Scots Greys are a very attractive and practical breed that deserves to be a lot more popular than it is. They are active birds that need a large outside run to keep fit and happy. If kept in a confined space they are inclined to fight and feather-peck each other. Beginners to poultry showing will find them fairly easy to manage and prepare for a show, there are no difficult features such as feathered feet, head crests or white ear lobes to cope with. A tidy Scots Grey has a good chance of winning a mixed 'AOV Light Breed' class at local shows away from the few areas where there are enough bred for show organizers to include classes for them in the show schedule.

SEBRIGHT (TRUE BANTAM)

Sir John Sebright, Baronet (a hereditary title) started to develop his breed of laced bantams in about 1800 at his estate at Markyate, near the Bedfordshire/Hertfordshire county boundary. Among the birds he used to make them were a Laced Poland, a Nankin Bantam and a smallish Henny Pit Game cock. Having started with Gold Laced Sebrights, he crossed some with a White Rosecomb cock he bought from London Zoo to make Silver Laced Sebrights. Some of his gentlemen friends took an interest, and they formed the Sebright Club about 1815. They held an annual show at the famous Gray's Inn Coffee House, Holborn, London on the first Tuesday in February. Sadly, the Sebright Club does not now have any records from these times, and the estate is now a private school, no longer owned by the Sebright family – so no, they are not in a box in the attic!

Artists of the time always depicted perfectly laced, tiny Sebright Bantams, so we do not know how good they really were by the time Sir John died in 1846, but they certainly are almost perfect now. They were originally intended to have a dark comb, wattles and facial skin, called 'mulberry' colour. This is still seen on females, but seldom on males, although they do at least have darkish coloured skin around their eyes. In order to maintain their perfect lacing and

Gold Sebright pair.

85

Silver Sebright female.

small size, most breeders keep closed flocks, which has led to a lot of infertility problems as a result of inbreeding. Some beginners have thought they could solve these problems by buying stock from several sources and crossing the strains in the belief that unrelated matings would improve fertility and vigour. This may be true, but the resulting Sebrights bred will probably be too large to show, have poor lacing and consequently be very difficult to sell or even give away. Young Sebrights cannot be assessed for lacing quality until mature as the details of their juvenile plumage will not necessarily be repeated in their first adult plumage. Lacing should ideally be the same thickness all round every feather; it often fades out along the sides. There should not be any 'mossiness', black speckles in the feather centres.

Sebrights were never intended to be practical bantams for the smallholding, but were rather delicate little gems for the connoisseur. The only beginners to poultry keeping likely to succeed with Sebrights are those with previous experience with other pets such as exotic aviary birds. Anyone else who is understandably attracted to their pretty laced plumage should consider Laced Wyandotte Bantams instead.

SHAMO (HARD FEATHER)

Shamo were developed as a fighting cock breed in Japan from birds imported from Thailand in the seventeenth century. They have only

Black-red Shamo male.

been bred in Europe since the 1980s, but were kept in the USA over a century ago. Some fanciers are fascinated by these prehistoric-looking birds, but their aggressive nature requires a lot of individual housing, so they are not suitable for beginners. Although they will usually fight each other on sight, they are generally very tame with people – so, surprising to some, a pair of Shamo could make excellent pets. Do not expect many eggs from a Shamo hen, and although the cocks would produce meaty table birds if crossed with other breeds, they are unlikely to do so as many are almost monogamous, often pairing with a single favourite hen.

They stand very upright, with the tail pointing down to the ground in a straight line with their back. Plumage is tight and scanty, with bare red skin showing along the breast bone and on the 'elbow' joints of their wings. Head characteristics are considered very important: thick beak, prominent eyebrow bones, a compact pea comb and a dewlapped throat instead of wattles. Shamo are not fully mature and showing all these features until two years old.

SILKIE (LIGHT SOFT FEATHER, LARGE AND BANTAM)

Historians today doubt whether the famous explorer Marco Polo (1254–1324) really visited all the places in China he described, he may have included stories from other travellers in his books; but he did describe Silkies, so either he or someone else must have seen them. Silkies may have been an old breed even then, so until more information becomes available, we do not know how ancient this unique breed really is. A few Silkies were brought to Europe and the Middle East over the centuries, where they were probably crossed with local chickens to make all the other crested breeds, but pure Silkies remained very much a rare curiosity until the late nineteenth century. One of the leading breeders in the early twentieth century was Mrs Adele Campbell who, in addition to being the Silkie Club's secretary for many years, also created the Campbell breed of duck. Silkies have been highly valued for their strong broody and maternal instincts, although chicks are sometimes lost by becoming tangled in their mother's fur-like plumage. To avoid this problem many hobbyists and gamekeepers who need broody bantams to hatch pheasant eggs use part Silkie crossbreds. Silkies, especially Whites, can be bathed and blow-dried to fluffy perfection – and regularly win major awards at the shows.

Until the 1980s there was just one size of Silkies, about halfway between the large fowl and bantam versions of other breeds. The American Poultry Association classified them as a bantam, whereas

White Silkie, large and bantam females.

the Poultry Club of Great Britain classed them as a large fowl. A few fanciers scattered around Europe made really tiny Silkie Bantams during the 1980s, which were such cute little things that they were soon becoming popular all over Europe, including the UK. This led to fanciers selecting for bigger large Silkies to emphasize the difference between them. It could be argued that these changes have led to the demise of the original medium-sized Silkie, which would be sad.

The five traditional colour varieties of Silkies are Black, Blue, Gold, Partridge and White. More varieties have been made in recent years, including patterns – which never really work with silkie plumage as has always been obvious on Partridge Silkies. All varietes of Silkies must have dark skin, a dull red shade, 'mulberry' is acceptable, but very dark blue, almost black, is preferred. Even the meat is this colour; it is considered a delicacy in China, but is rather less popular in the West. All plumage must be silkie, some birds failing by having almost normal wing and tail feathers. There are yet more unusual features: a fluffy crest, a compact 'cushion' comb, turquoise-blue ear lobes, feathered legs and feet and an extra hind toe on each foot. Silkies can either have normal wattles or be bearded.

Silkies are popular with everyone from beginners to life-long poultry keepers. White Silkies need a lot of expert care and attention if they are to be show winners – they could be regarded as the poultry equivalent of Poodles in the dog world. We have all seen the difference between a pet Poodle and a show Poodle (which, don't forget, is a pet as well) – the same applies to White Silkies. Some strains of Silkies are very susceptible to Marek's disease, and they all seem susceptible to scaly leg mite infestation. It would be advisable to buy from an expert breeder, and aim to provide similar housing and care.

SPANISH (RARE BREED, LARGE AND BANTAM)

Their ancestors may have come from Spain, but the white-faced Spanish breed was initially created in The Netherlands (under Spanish rule until 1700), and then refined and developed in England, particularly in London and Bristol. Their unique white faces were gradually made bigger and bigger by two centuries of selective breeding. They can lose a lot of body heat through their white facial skin, which is one reason why they were mainly bred in city gardens in the south of England, rather than on farms in colder areas. Groups

Spanish male.

of enthusiasts in these two cities held private shows long before the first general poultry show in 1845. Although they were a popular show and laying breed in the mid-nineteenth century, they gradually declined, almost to extinction. A few enthusiasts in England and Germany revived the breed from the few remaining birds in the 1970s, but they remain very much a Rare Breed.

Spanish Bantams have been made several times since the first attempt in the 1800s, only to die out each time. The current strain bred in limited, but slightly safer, numbers all over Europe was created by Kent-based Rare Breed expert Fred Hams in the 1980s.

Black has always been the main, usually the only, colour variety, but Blues and Whites have appeared from time to time over the last 150+ years. Their faces need a fair amount of special care and show preparation (baby powder), and they need protection from cold winds. Even with ideal housing and care, Spanish cocks seldom survive three winters, although the hens are much hardier and long-lived. Most people who keep Spanish do not have very many other breeds, and their other breeds are usually simpler, less time-consuming types.

SULTAN (RARE BREED)

Sultans were said to have been kept as garden pets in the Sultan of Constantinople's (now Istanbul) palace. Some of their ancestors were almost certainly White Silkies imported from China. They became known to Europeans after a crate of them was sent to Miss

Sultan male.

Elizabeth Watts of Hampstead, London in January 1854. A few more were sent to England over the following decades, but not many. The same can be said of the number of people keeping them – Sultans have always been an exotic rarity. There are probably more flocks of Sultans now than at any time since 1854. One of the early (*circa* 1890–1930) Sultan breeders was Mrs Adele Campbell (*see* Silkies). A few attempts have been made to produce Sultan Bantams but, surprisingly for such an ornamental breed, they have never been properly established. This may be because large Sultans are quiet, docile and not very big, so everyone concerned has been content with them.

They are a very 'high maintenance' breed, having a head crest, beard, white plumage and heavily feathered legs and feet. Sultans also have an unusual horned comb and an extra hind toe on each foot. Houses must be regularly cleaned and must be big enough to keep them inside for much of the time, although Sultans will benefit from time out on your lawn on nice days. They are not suitable for most beginners, although someone who has kept another type of specialist pet, a Persian cat for example, is likely to appreciate the care that Sultans need.

SUMATRA (RARE BREED, LARGE AND BANTAM)

This is another breed that was developed a long way away from its nominal place of origin. Mr Butters of Roxbury, Massachusetts, imported some fighting cocks from Sumatra in 1847, but the long-tailed exhibition breed he and subsequent fanciers created from them is quite different. They were first called 'Sumatra Game', but the 'Game' was dropped to emphasize the fact that they are now very much a fancy long-tailed breed, not a fighter. Frederick Heaton of Norwich imported the first Sumatras to England from Toronto, Canada in 1901 or 1902. There have been several strains of Sumatra Bantams made since the 1920s in England, Germany, The Netherlands and the USA. Sumatras are also one of the breeds that have been bred in greater numbers and better quality in recent years than at any time in the past.

Blue Sumatra male.

Black Sumatra female.

Their general shape and style is usually described as 'pheasant-like', having a long tail that extends horizonally in line with the bird's back. For most of their 160-year history only Black Sumatras were recognized, but Blues and Whites have been made since the 1980s. All three colour varieties should have dark facial skin. Dark red is acceptable, it is often as dark as you can get on cocks, but very dark blue, almost black, skin is preferable. Black Sumatra females are most likely to have the darkest faces, and often win 'Best of Breed' as a result.

Sumatras are active birds, and obviously have long tails, so their housing must allow for their needs. They need generous-sized outside runs with high fences and large houses with high perches well away from the house walls, so they do not break those tail feathers. The hens are excellent broodies and mothers, so any that are not up to show and breeding quality will still be very useful for hatching the eggs of any other breeds you keep. Sumatras are one of the more exotic-looking breeds that are still within the capabilities of most novice poultry keepers, as long as you can provide suitable accommodation for them.

SUSSEX (HEAVY SOFT FEATHER, LARGE AND BANTAM)

Although they were bred in Kent, Surrey and Sussex for centuries, the Sussex breed is not mentioned in Victorian poultry books. This is because the experts then regarded them as Dorking crosses. Local farmers knew better however, and eventually established their breed by forming the Sussex Poultry Club at the Elephant and Castle Hotel, Lewes, Sussex on 23 July 1903. They initially recognized three colour varieties: Light, Speckled and 'Red or Brown'. The latter were redefined as two separate varieties by 1913. Buff Sussex (with the same black neck, wing and tail markings as Lights) and White Sussex were added during the 1920s; Silver Sussex in 1948, and Coronation Sussex (as Light Sussex, but with blue instead of black markings) are a very new addition. Sussex Bantams were first made in the 1920s, with the newer colours obviously being added later.

Large Light Sussex were by far the most commercially important variety, especially from 1920 until 1960, when thousands of British farmers mated RIR cocks with Light Sussex hens, a sex-linked cross that gave brown pullets for laying and white cockerels for table bird rearing. Different exhibition and utility strains of Light Sussex were created, the exhibition birds being larger (but poorer layers) and

Light Sussex trio.

Speckled Sussix trio.

with better-defined markings than the utility type. Both types are still available, and it is up to today's hobby poultry keepers to decide which would best suit their needs. It is quite wrong to say that one is 'better' than the other – they each do what they are intended to do: win prizes or lay eggs.

Sussex have a smallish single comb, normal wattles, red ear lobes and white shanks and feet. They are solidly built birds with a full, rounded breast and a long flat back. Lights are still the most popular variety, so stock for sale should be easy to locate. Lights and Whites must be perfectly clean if they are to have any chance of winning at a show, so novice exhibitors might be wise to choose one of the darker varieties. Speckleds and Buffs are readily available, and both are very pretty. Brown, Coronation, Red and Silver Sussex are all comparatively rare, but all are interesting and attractive if there are any breeders who live near enough for you to visit to buy some. There are quite a lot of Sussex specialists who keep several colour varieties, but do not try to keep the whole set – it would involve keeping far too many birds for even the most enthusiastic person with a farm to keep them all on. Large Sussex are really big birds, which need large houses and eat a lot of food. Just one variety, if a top-quality flock is intended, will be enough for most hobbyists. A collection of two or three colours of Sussex Bantams would be more viable.

TRANSYLVANIAN NAKED NECK
(RARE BREED, LARGE AND BANTAM)

Transylvania is a region of Romania, but Naked Necks are known to have been bred in many parts of central and southern Europe, the Middle East, and all around the Mediterranean. There are now many thousands of naked-necked broiler hybrids reared annually in these countries, where they are comfortable in the warm conditions and then easily hand plucked – many consumers in these countries still prefer to buy their chickens alive and do the necessary deed themselves. Exhibition Naked Necks have been more popular in Germany and Austria than anywhere else since first shown by Herr Weber at Vienna in 1875, and as Transylvania was then part of the Austro-Hungarian Empire their breed name is historically justifiable. In all other countries Naked Necks have always been an unusual novelty. We are accustomed to seeing a few at the shows, but it is difficult to imagine what rows and rows of them, such as the 110 Naked Necks entered in the 1907 Leipzig Show, would have looked like. Naked Neck Bantams were first made by German fancier Karl Huth in the 1920s, but current strains are believed to have been made, also in Germany, in the 1950s.

The naked-necked broilers and some Naked Necks seen at the shows outside Germany have a clump of feathers about halfway down the front of their neck, but good quality exhibition Naked Necks have completely bare necks. The neck skin should ideally be bright red, which is maintained by giving them constant access to outside runs, and hence sunlight. The neck skin fades to pale pink if they are kept inside. Naked Necks also have far fewer body feathers

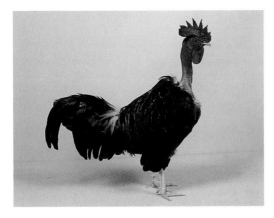

Black-red Transylvanian Naked Neck bantam male.

Lavender Transylvanian Naked Neck bantam female.

than normal chickens, but despite this are perfectly happy in all but the coldest climates. Although they have existed, patterned plumage never really looks right on Naked Necks, so self colours, Black, Blue, Buff, Red and White, are most popular.

Their unusual appearance means they are never going to be in 'the top ten' of favourite breeds, but there will always be a minority who are fascinated by them. Naked Neck baby chicks are especially weird. If you like them, Naked Necks are good layers and make docile, friendly pets.

VORWERK (RARE BREED, LARGE AND BANTAM)

Oscar Vorwerk of Hamburg-Othmarschen, Germany made these between 1902 and 1912 from crosses of Lakenvelders, utility-type

Buff Orpingtons and Buff Ramelslohers, a German breed. Vorwerk Bantams were made in the 1950s. Large Vorwerks were first imported to the UK in the late 1970s, the bantams about 1990.

Vorwerks have the same unusual plumage pattern as Lakenvelders, a solid black neck and tail and black wing markings, in this case contrasting with a 'buff' (warm ochre shade) body. There is also a new variety with a blue instead of black neck and tail. As with Lakenvelders, the ideal demarcation of the black/buff or blue/buff parts is seldom achieved. Birds that are naturally 'nearly right' are routinely improved by the careful removal of the most obvious wrong-coloured feathers for showing.

In addition to being very pretty, Vorwerks are a docile and productive breed that would be an excellent choice for anyone who

Vorwerk male.

Vorwerk female.

lives near enough to one of the few existing breeders to buy them. There will inevitably be quite a lot of mismarked surplus cockerels bred each season, so a pragmatic attitude to culling and eating home-reared stock is essential.

WELSUMMER (LIGHT SOFT FEATHER, LARGE AND BANTAM)

This is one of the most popular breeds with hobbyist poultry keepers because they lay rich brown-shelled eggs, and they look exactly as everyone imagines a traditional farmyard chicken should look. In fact they are a comparatively recent creation, first exhibited at the World Poultry Congress at The Hague in 1921. They had been developed over the previous decade at Welsum, a village to the north-east of Barneveld, the centre of the Dutch poultry industry. The breed name is Welsumer, with one 'm', in The Netherlands and some other countries. Welsummers were rather slimmer in general build when they were first imported to the UK in the 1920s, which is why they were put in the Light Breeds section. There is very little difference today in the size and shape of Welsummers from Barnevelders and Marans, both of which are classed as Heavy Breeds, so it might be time for the PCGB Council to reconsider. Welsummer Bantams were first made in the 1930s, but they did not lay the vitally important brown eggs until about 1960. As a result, Welsummer Bantams have been gradually increasing in popularity since then.

Welsummers have a modest-sized single comb, normal wattles and red ear lobes. Show birds should have red eyes. Light eye colour

Welsummer bantam male.

Welsummer female.

is a common fault, but this does not matter if they are to be kept at home as layers. The main plumage colour is a modified Black-red/Partridge pattern. Males have brown mixed in with their otherwise black breast feathering, which is a show fault on most other black-red breeds. Females are generally darker shades of gold, brown and salmon than other Partridge breeds, but in this case the darker shades contrast with light gold feather shafts over their back and wings. Similarly modified versions of Silver Duckwing and Gold Duckwing patterns are recognized in some countries, but are rare. If they have not been made already, there is probably someone, somewhere, working on Blue-red/Partridge Welsummers. Also, *see* Welbars in the Autosexing Breeds section.

As with other dark-brown egg breeds, be aware that shell colour lightens through the spring and summer, with the best layers fading more than the poor layers. Be careful when choosing which eggs to incubate that you do not either end up with a strain that lays very dark eggs, but not many of them, or good layers of light-coloured eggs. Try to keep a balance.

WYANDOTTE (HEAVY SOFT FEATHER, LARGE AND BANTAM)

Developed in the north-eastern states of the USA, Wyandottes are one of the most popular pure breeds all over the world. There are lots of colour varieties in both sizes to choose from, they are easy to keep, the hens go broody and are good mothers, and they still provide a challenge for exhibitors. It may be easy to breed Wyandottes generally, but a lot of expertise is needed to breed and prepare Wyandottes good enough to win a class at the major shows.

When peace returned to America in 1865, after the Civil War, several poultry breeders had a similar idea: to create a fairly large, useful breed with the pretty lacing then only available on exotic Polands and tiny Sebright Bantams. Each breeder had his own name for the breed they were trying to make, and they differed in details such as comb type and clean/feathered legs. As they were still arguing when they first applied for standardization by the American Poultry Association in 1872, they were refused. They sorted themselves out, and agreed the name Wyandottes, which was recognized by the APA in 1883. 'Wyandotte' is usually mentioned in poultry books as the name of a tribe of Native Americans (the name Hurons actually called themselves), but it was also the name of a ship owned by the family of Fred Houdlette, one of the breeders – which was probably more significant in deciding the matter. Gold Laced Wyandottes followed shortly afterwards, then Blue Laced and Buff Laced. Several breeds had been used to make these varieties, so it is not surprising that some different colours appeared for some time, including Blacks and Whites. Both needed a few years of selecting breeding to properly establish these varieties, the first chicks having some odd-coloured feathers.

Another group of breeders thought it would be a good idea to make a breed with the attractive markings of Partridge Cochins and Dark Brahmas, but without feathered feet. When they saw how popular Laced Wyandottes were becoming they selected the rose-combed birds among their flocks and applied to the APA to have them recognized as Partridge and Silver Pencilled Wyandottes. Barred Wyandottes were made in Germany. Wyandotte Bantams in these and other colours were made by various fanciers in America, Germany and the UK between 1900 and 1930.

Wyandottes are a hardy breed in cold climates as they have compact rose combs and a thick coat of feathers. This was a deliberate intention on the part of the originators, many of whom lived in New York State, Massachusetts and Wisconsin, where the winters are very cold indeed. They were primarily intended to be plump-bodied table birds, so are not the best layers. This is particularly noticeable in the large fowl, which lay rather smaller eggs than you would hope for from such big hens. They were also intended to be pretty birds (hence the Laced and Partridge/Pencilled patterns) suitable for a country gentlemen's estate, a role for which they are still perfect. Good trios of these varieties attract brisk bidding at poultry auctions. White and Black Wyandottes became favourites among expert show exhibitors. The combinations of snow-white plumage and bright yellow shanks/feet or glossy black plumage and bright yellow shanks/feet are not easily achieved. Fewer of today's newcomers to our hobby seem interested in these two varieties, but as really good White and Black Wyandottes are usually contenders for 'Best in Show' awards they deserve consideration by anyone who would like to have a full trophy cabinet. If showable Laced and Partridge/Pencilled Wyandottes are to be bred, the breed standards and the relevant aspects of poultry genetics must be closely studied. More detail can be found in *Exhibition Poultry Keeping* (David Scrivener, The Crowood Press), particularly the Genetics and Double Mating chapters. Some readers might be thinking, 'I don't intend showing, so it doesn't matter if the markings on my birds are not exactly as the show judges require.' It may not matter to you, but potential customers of any surplus stock you breed and hope to sell will only be interested in birds that are at least reasonably close to standard colour and shape.

They are fairly docile and easy to keep, so are a good choice for beginners. It will be at least six months, probably a year, before

Silver Laced Wyandotte bantam quartet.

Partridge Wyandotte bantam trio, UK-standard exhibition male and cock-breeder females.

novice breeders have reared a batch of young birds to be selected. This gives plenty of time to study more detailed books, Wyandotte Club literature and so on to learn which birds to keep and breed from.

YOKOHAMA (RARE BREED, LARGE AND BANTAM)

These are often called 'Japanese Long-tailed Fowl', which is almost, but not exactly correct. There are several long-tailed breeds in Japan (Minohiki, Onagadori, Satsumadori and Totenko), but none called 'Yokohama'. This name was used by European importers because stock came in ships that had set out from the port of Yokohama in the late nineteenth century. Communication and translation difficulties seem to have prevented the first breeders in England, France and Germany from learning the proper Japanese names and breed

Red Saddled White Yokohama male.

Silver Duckwing Yokohama male.

details, so they invented their own. German breeders classed them as two breeds, only calling the gamier pea- and walnut-combed bird 'Jokohamas' (probably a mix of Minohikis and Satsumadori), and inventing the name 'Phönix' for the single-combed type (probably a mix of Onagadori and Totenko). More details of all these varieties can be found in *Rare Poultry Breeds* (David Scrivener, The Crowood Press).

It needs more expertise than beginners are likely to have to breed and prepare top-quality long-tails for exhibition, but a lot of people keep them as exotic gardens pets. Their tail feathers are virtually certain to get broken and dirty under normal conditions, although it helps if they are provided with large houses, with fairly high perches (about a metre), placed well away from the house walls. Many of the birds for sale at poultry auctions are 'between size', too big to be a bantam, too small to be a large fowl. If you are starting with stock like this, you should select for size (bigger or smaller, as you wish) as well as length of tail and saddle feathers. Those who would like to show them should speak to, and preferably visit, one of the experienced breeders whom they will no doubt meet when attending a show.

Silver Grey Dorkings by J.W. Ludlow, circa 1912.

— 3 —

Commercial Hybrids

The modern poultry industry, which perhaps should be thought of as the egg production industry and the broiler chicken industry as they are separate entities, started to develop in America during the 1920s and 1930s. Poultry gradually ceased to be a minor part of general farming, and 'dual-purpose breeds' began to lose ground to large flocks of small-bodied White Leghorns kept by egg producers and equally large flocks of crossbred table chickens (White Cornish x Rhode Island Red, White Cornish x New Hampshire Red or White Cornish x White Plymouth Rock).

These changes did not happen in the UK until the 1950s and early 1960s, where the sex-linked Rhode Island Red x Light Sussex cross remained the poultry farmers' favourite. This was partly a result of British consumers' preference for brown-shelled eggs, and partly a result of grain shortages that continued to affect the UK long after the end of the Second World War. One thing was common to both countries, poultry farmers had lost their previous connection and affection for 'pure breeds'. Owners of large flocks were mainly interested in maximum growth rate and egg production from each ton of chicken feed used. They no longer entered poultry shows, and did not care about the details of their birds' appearance.

Throughout the period from 1920 to 1960 there were rapid strides in the science of genetics, and much of the research was being done on chickens. This was because chickens are an economically important species, and are smaller, cheaper and have a shorter life cycle than large farm livestock. They are the ideal subject for applied scientists who have to justify the considerable costs of large-scale experimental breeding programmes and the production performannce test flocks of each mating tried.

John Kimber, who started a hatchery at Fremont, California in 1934, revolutionized poultry breeding by introducing the first hybrid layers. He first developed a number of carefully pedigree bred strains of White Leghorns, all of which were inbred; as a result they were good, but not really good layers themselves. He then tried various crosses between these strains, finding that some of these matings produced layers that were spectacularly good. The term 'nicked' was coined for the successful strain crosses; which were then sold as the first commercial hybrid layers. You will note that they were not crossbreeds, only White Leghorns were involved. His birds laid much better than anyone else's White Leghorns because they maximized the 'hybrid vigour effect' from certain combinations of inbred strains. If his hybrid-bred White Leghorns were then bred from, much of the benefit would be lost. Birds bred from them might still be pretty good producers, but not as good as the hybrids he sold. In order for customers to keep coming back for more, all hybrid breeding companies since then have been very protective and secretive towards their 'parent' and 'grandparent' strains.

The scientific principle behind this system of crossing inbred strains was that most harmful genes are recessive. Many genes consist of the 'program' for making chemicals needed for an aspect of the body's metabolism. Defective genes simple fail to function, but only one of the two genes for each allele is defective, the 'good one' can make enough of the relevant chemical for the chicken (or other animal or plant) to function normally. The most successful crosses between inbred strains are those where each of the two strains had different defective genes, so all metabolism functions are covered by a good gene from at least one parent.

Once Kimber Farms had established the principle with White Leghorn-based layers, other companies followed with hybrid types of broiler chickens and brown egg layers, which did involve more than one breed. Over the intervening decades poultry breeding companies have developed their own versions of breeds in their top-security breeding establishments. Their Barred Rocks, Light Sussex, New Hampshire Reds, Rhode Island Reds, White Cornish and White Rocks are very different from the breeds of the same names seen at poultry shows. There will also be considerable differences between strains within a breed because specific strains are bred for particular characteristics. The same principle of trying various crosses of inbred strains to find a combination which 'nicks' is applied.

'Hybrids', in this context (as opposed to sterile hybrids between different species of animals or plants), are perfectly fertile and can be bred from, but the resulting offspring will be rather variable in terms of performance levels, disease resistance and so on even though they might look fairly uniform. Hobbyist poultry keepers often try breeding from them, perhaps by mating brown-egg layer hybrids with Marans or Welsummer males. The pullets so bred will probably perform well enough in a back garden context, but do not get carried away with dreams of making your own 'new breed'. Hybrid breeding is a very high-tech, very expensive process, and every aspect of each hybrid can be predicted with amazing accuracy as long as they are kept in proper conditions. As they say on some TV shows, 'Do not try this at home.'

Since 2000 a number of hybrids have come on the market that have been specifically made for organic, free range, commercial producers and home poultry keepers. They include some blue-egg layers. Many of them have been given names that can cause beginners to confuse them with traditional breeds. Some are detailed here, with the production levels they are capable of achieving with ideal housing, feeding and care. If your birds fail to perform as well, it is probably your fault, not the breeder's. The author does not recommend one above another of the hybrids detailed below as examples; simply go for the best value for money among the hybrids available at your local supplier.

Hybrids are the best option for most back garden poultry keepers, especially the many who are unable to keep cockerels. Hybrid layer cockerel chicks are routinely killed at the hatchery, with some being sold (frozen) to zoos and private keepers of reptiles, falcons and so on. These cockerels are slow-growing, and never make good table birds, so are not worth rearing. Hybrid pullets lay more eggs than pure breeds and are much cheaper to buy. Few pure breed hobbyists will sell pullets without cockerels anyway.

Black Rock layers.

BLACK ROCK

Commercial Black Rock layers are the result of a sex-linked cross between Rhode Island Red males and Barred Rock females. Both parent breeds and the resulting Black Rock pullets are very different from the versions of the same breeds you will see at poultry shows. These Black Rocks have mostly black plumage with some golden-brown on the head, neck and (on some of them) breast feathering. If properly kept they should lay about 280 brown eggs in their first year. They have been selected for hardiness in free-range conditions by the Muirfield Hatchery, Kinross, Scotland, who have agents around the country.

Hebden Black.

HEBDEN BLACK

This is fairly similar to the Black Rock above, bred by Calder Valley Breeders Ltd, Hebden Bridge, Yorkshire and Cyril Bason (Stokesay) Ltd, Craven Arms, Shropshire. Any differences between these two in terms of egg numbers, egg size, food consumption and so on may be apparent to commercial producers with thousands of birds, but are unlikely to be noticeable to those with a dozen or so in their garden.

CALDER RANGER

Also produced by Calder Valley Breeders and Cyril Bason, this is a typical light brown feathered hybrid layer in general appearance. It

Calder Ranger.

is slightly smaller than the two above, and so has slightly lower feed consumption. Calder Rangers, like other hybrids of similar appearance, are suitable for free-range or any commercial intensive system, although they may not do quite as well as the two above on free range in very open, windswept situations. In appropriate conditions, and with correct housing, feeding and so on, they can lay over 315 eggs in their first year. Their eggs are brown, but a lighter shade than those of Black Rocks or Hebden Blacks.

SPECKLEDY

Also produced by Calder Valley Breeders and Cyril Bason, this hybrid is partly bred from Cuckoo Marans, which it broadly resembles. Speckledy hens can lay 260–270 dark brown eggs under good

Speckledy.

management in their first year. Pure bred Cuckoo Marans lay darker brown eggs, but rather fewer of them. This hybrid has been developed for free range or 'barn' (what were called 'deep litter') systems. A lot of people keeping Speckledy hens have no doubt then bought a Cuckoo Marans cockerel and bred from them. This is a perfectly understandable thing to do as long as the cockerels bred from them are all eaten and the pullets carefully identified (with leg rings) and kept for home egg production. Such crosses must not be sold as 'Marans' or 'Speckledys' as they are neither. 'Speckledy' is a registered trade name of the two breeding companies, and any competent show judge will know that they are not proper Marans and disqualify them, thus upsetting buyers who bought them as 'Marans' and tried showing them.

ISA BROWN, ISA WARREN AND SHAVER BROWN

All three of these are brown-egg laying hybrids sold by the Tom Barron ISA company. They all have bright orange-red plumage with white underfluff, tail and wings. Under expert management they can lay about 350 eggs in a 62-week production period from 18 to 80 weeks of age. This number of eggs may only be possible with birds housed in buildings with electric lighting to provide greater day length during autumn, winter and early spring.

DOMINANT CZ HYBRIDS

This company, based in the Czech Republic, has agents in the UK and other countries that supply an unusual range of hybrids that, because of their interesting colours, are likely to appeal to hobbyist poultry keepers. Not all local agents may sell the whole range, but there is a good chance that all of them will have enough for those intending to buy twenty or so pullets to have a few of each of several kinds.

Dominant Brown D-102 Brown-egg layers similar in appearance and production levels to the ISAs and Shavers mentioned above. They are bred from commercial versions of Rhode Island Red males and Rhode Island White females.

Dominant Sussex D-104 These have the same plumage pattern as Light Sussex but are smaller than exhibition-type large Light

D - 102

PARENTS   ♂ ♀   HYBRID

D - 192

PARENTS   ♂ ♀   HYBRID

D - 109

PARENTS   ♂ ♀   HYBRID

D - 107

PARENTS   ♂ ♀   HYBRID

D - 149

PARENTS ♂ ♀ HYBRID

D - 104

PARENTS HYBRID

D - 959

PARENTS HYBRID

D - 843

PARENTS HYBRID

Sussex and have yellow shanks and feet instead of the white shanks/feet of standard Sussex. They are attractive birds, and lay many more brown eggs than exhibition Sussex, but would not be recognized as a Sussex at all in a show.

Dominant Blue D-107 These hybrids have interesting bluish grey plumage and lay brown eggs. They are bred from 'Splash' males (white and a few black or grey feathers) and Cuckoo hens (Marans colour).

Dominant Black D-109 These hens have mostly black plumage with some golden brown on the head and neck, therefore looking very similar to the Black Rock and Hebden Black hybrids mentioned above. D-109s lay dark-brown eggs.

Dominant Black D-149 These hens are mostly black with some silvery white head and neck feathering. They are bred from Light Sussex colour males and Cuckoo hens. Like all hybrid breeding companies, Dominant CZ do not say how many closed breeding strains they have, or which strains are used to make which hybrids. So the Light Sussex coloured birds used to breed D-149s may, or may not, be the same ones used for breeding D-104s. D-149s lay dark-brown eggs.

Dominant Brown D-192 The brown-egg-laying hybrids have golden brown plumage with black tail, wings and some Black neck stripes. They are similar in colour to standard bred New Hampshire Reds, but have a smaller body and longer tail. The parents are Rhode Island Red coloured males and Light Sussex coloured females.

Dominant Partridge D-300 These are very pretty patterned hens with white ear lobes, laying white or light brown eggs. They are similar in appearance to Brown Leghorn hens. Hobbyists with a flock of D-300s who would like to try breeding from them will obviously prefer to use a Brown Leghorn cock if they can obtain one. They must be honest about the parentage of any birds they sell from this mating as it would be unethical to sell them as 'Brown Leghorns', especially to anyone who might be breeding further generations from them. However, if Brown Leghorn x D-300 pullets are then mated to pure Brown Leghorn males, the ¾ Brown Leghorns might be the foundation of a useful new strain of this now worryingly rare old breed.

Dominant Amber D-843 These hens have mostly white plumage, with some golden feathers on their wings and back. They lay dark-brown eggs. The males used to breed them have white plumage, and the females are golden-brown with black tail, wings and neck striping. The breeds used to make these parent strains are a closely guarded commercial secret. One could guess that the dark-brown-egg genes may come from Welsummers or White Barnevelders, that were then crossed with more conventional commercial egg hybrid breeding strains to raise egg numbers.

Dominant Barred D-959 This is a dark-brown-egg laying, cuckoo-barred plumaged hybrid similar in appearance to the Speckledy mentioned above. As with Speckledy hens, hobbyists are likely to try breeding from them using Cuckoo Marans cocks, but it would be unethical to sell the resulting Marans x D-959 crosses as 'Marans'. Unlike the Brown Leghorn/D-300 example mentioned above, there is no shortage of proper Cuckoo Marans, so no conservation need to make new strains.

— 4 —
Housing

Contrary to some people's assumptions, keepers of pure breeds of chickens and bantams are not necessarily enthusiasts of 'free range' systems. Certainly many are, and they will probably keep those breeds that really need access to large grassed runs to keep happy and healthy, Derbyshire Redcaps and Welsummers for example. However, breeds with heavily feathered feet, head crests and those with white plumage will need more controlled conditions if these features are to be kept in showable condition. Show exhibitors keep their birds, usually in small groups, in generous-sized houses because they are only allowed outside on dry days.

Not many hobbyists have enough space to allow their birds to be permanently outside without their runs rapidly becoming stripped to bare earth, which in the winter becomes foul-smelling mud. In these circumstances, the main priority must be to conserve the limited area of grass available, usually by having several housed groups share one run on a rota basis.

The threat of Avian Influenza and other serious poultry diseases, with the requirement that all poultry be kept under cover (to avoid contact with wild birds that might be infected) during an outbreak, is a real challenge to some free-range poultry keepers. It is not a problem for competent pure-breed enthusiasts as they have enough housing to keep their birds inside anyway, even those with breeds that are normally running outside every day.

There are several basic types of poultry housing, ranging from large sheds divided into pens to small movable arks. All systems can be used by pure-breed fanciers, their relative value depending on the breeds involved. Arks and smaller houses may be bought from one of the manufacturers who advertise in the poultry and smallholding magazines, or they may be home-made by DIYers. Larger sheds may be converted from existing buildings, or built from scratch.

Whichever housing systems are used, pure breed flocks, especially if shown, will be divided into many small groups, including some pairs and individually penned cockerels. Novice fanciers

Group of houses for feather-footed or crested breeds that are allowed to run out on grass in rotation, weather permitting.

Pair of houses with aviary-type runs, necessary for active breeds that would fly out of open runs, and for rearing young bantams safe from cats and birds of prey. The partition would need to be solid along the lower 60cm if both runs contained aggressive cockerels.

117

should also remember that a hen-house advertised as being suitable for twenty-five layers (hybrids) will only be suitable for about eight of the larger heavy breeds. New poultry houses are quite expensive, and the nest boxes and perches are often unsuitable for long-tailed and very large pure breeds, so it may be both cheaper and better to buy a garden shed from your local DIY or garden centre and adapt it. This should be within the capabilities of even the worst carpenters.

In addition to housing for adult birds and larger growers, a large shed will also be needed for chick rearing, storage of poultry food (in rodent-proof containers) and carrying boxes, plus some show cages or equivalent-sized pens for assessing and training your birds.

POULTRY HOUSE 'FURNITURE'

Pen Partitions

If a large shed is to be built, or an existing building converted, to contain several breeding pens, the pen partitions should be solid from the floor up to above the cockerel's head height, with the top part of the partition consisting of wire netting. Perches should be placed well away from the partitions, or neighbouring cockerels may spend all day on the perches, pecking at each other through the wire. Pen doors should be of the same lower half solid (plywood), upper half mesh, design, and should not go down to the floor. At floor level, there should be a 6 inch (15cm) board nailed across from post to post. This is because the pen floors are normally covered with litter, straw or wood shavings that would jam the bottom of the doors.

Perches

The ideal height for perches is just above the cockerel's head height for most breeds. Long-tailed breeds need higher perches, high enough for their tails not to touch the floor. Indian Game / Cornish, susceptible to leg and foot injuries because of their weight, have low perches, only about a foot (30cm) high. Japanese (Chabo) bantams and breeds with heavy foot-feathering are not usually allowed perches at all; so regular replacement of floor litter is essential. Large breeds really need wider perches, about 2½ inches (6.5cm), than those in most commercially made poultry houses.

Interior of house painted white and with ample mesh-covered windows to give light and air to birds. Note plastic drum-type nest box inside.

Nest Boxes

If you have a commercially made hen-house with integral nest boxes, you will obviously use them, but if building a house yourself, or adapting another building, there are a lot of advantages to having loose single nest boxes. Suitably sized plastic drums with a hole cut in the side are excellent, their inside surfaces being smooth and washable. When attempting to find appropriate containers, you should obviously read the label to check that the original contents were not toxic or otherwise too dangerous for you to do the necessary washing out and cutting to transform it into a nest box. It is normal to lay the container on its side, and place a brick in front of the opening you have cut out.

If no plastic drums are available, suitable nest boxes can be made from plywood. If the breeds you keep are non-sitters, they can be made in blocks of two, three or four, but for breeds who do go broody, single boxes are best. When a hen has shown signs of being broody for a couple of days she can be moved in the nest in which she has already happily settled to a small pen where she can do her sitting in peace. Strong cardboard boxes are also useful as nest boxes, used for a month or two, and then disposed of. Their temporary nature may be a good red mite control measure.

As hens often scratch nesting material around, often down to the hard floor of the box, it is a good idea to put a newspaper or paper feed sack in the bottom of each nest. This can prevent egg breakages. Then put in a layer of wood shavings, and then hay and/or straw

119

made into a nest shape, which the hens will happily adjust for their maximum comfort.

Floor Litter

Wood shavings, bought in compacted, plastic-covered bales from most animal feed suppliers, are the main material used. Those on friendly terms with the owner of a carpentry workshop may be able to get some free, but may have to bag it themselves. In this case, only take softwood (light-coloured) shavings as (red) hardwood shavings give rise to give choking clouds of dust, and stain white plumage. A few red shavings mixed with mostly 'white' shavings will be OK.

Wheat straw is another traditional litter material, cheaper than buying bales of shavings, and is excellent for adult turkeys, chickens and the larger breeds of bantams, but will mat down and get damp if used for small bantams and young stock. Do not use straw for feather-legged breeds as it will break their foot feathers.

Dry fallen leaves can be collected in the autumn, but are also only suitable for birds large and active enough to scratch it around. Again, do not use it for small bantams, feather-legged birds or white-plumaged birds. Stock for whom it is suitable will greatly enjoy scratching in leaves, as they will probably find juicy insects and other tasty morsels.

Feeders and Drinkers

There are several types of both on the market, but when chickens are to be kept in very small groups there is a lot to be said in favour of plastic dog bowls from your local pet shop, or even some suitable ceramic (heavier than plastic, more difficult for chickens to tip over) bowls you might find at your local car boot sale.

Simple bowls or troughs are good for food if combined with an evening routine of emptying them back into your feed bucket when you shut your birds in for the night and collect the day's eggs. There are tube feeders and other designs that will hold enough food for a week, but these are likely to attract rats and mice.

Fount drinkers rely on a partial vacuum to hold the reserve of water in, releasing enough to keep the trough around the base topped up. For many years they were made of galvanized steel, the 'Eltex' brand being the most often seen in the UK. They are still made, but the plastic models now made are much cheaper. Available in a range of sizes, the smaller ones can be placed on the pen floor for chicks (under a lamp or with a hen), but larger models used for

Plastic drum-type nest box, two plastic drinkers, three types (two of each) of hook-on feed or water pots for use with individually housed birds (show training and so on), and four assorted troughs and bowls for feed that should be emptied every evening so no food is left overnight to attract rats and mice.

adults are best placed on some bricks or concrete blocks to keep the water cleaner.

Some breeds need specific types of food and water containers, Polish and others with large feathered crests, Leghorns and Minorcas with very large combs, and tall breeds like Modern Game that have to be kept in the habit of standing well up for the judge. All food and water containers should have a smooth edge, beard feathers and wattles can be damaged if caught by cracks on a sharp edge.

RUN FENCING

Your external perimeter fence must be capable of not only keeping your birds in, but also keeping predators out. In the UK this can be difficult enough, and we have only badgers, foxes and the smaller (but equally dangerous) Mustelidae species: stoats, mink and escaped ferrets. We should spare a thought for fanciers who have to keep wolves – and worse – at bay in other countries.

The external fence should ideally be at least 7 feet (2m) high, which is fairly obvious; but less obvious, and equally (if not more) important is the bottom of the fence. All of our native and feral predators will try to dig their way in, so the fence should extend underground a foot (30cm) or so if possible. The top half of the fence will normally be wire netting, but it is preferable to have the lower half solid, which both acts as a windbreak and helps to lessen interest in your birds from badgers and foxes. Remember the motto – to see is to want. Fanciers in the suburbs may imagine this doesn't apply to them, but it does. There are many foxes living right in the heart of our largest cities, and they seem to be bolder and more determined than their country cousins.

Internal fences, between runs, should not need to be quite as secure, but the securer the better: if a fox gets past the outer fence, one of the pen divisions might make a difference between a minor disaster and a major one. Cockerels can seriously damage each other by fighting through wire netting, so all pen dividing fences must be solid to above their head height, which also further reduces wind chill. Internal fences must, of course, be high enough to prevent birds from flying over. Heavy breeds of chickens will often stay where they should be with fencing only 4 feet (120cm) high.

Buying Poultry Houses and Arks

There are many designs on the market, sometimes with considerable price differences between manufacturers for similar units. Plywood constructed houses are often cheaper than tongued and grooved or feather-edged boarded ones. Plywood may not look as attractive, but is more practical, being less draughty, stronger and gives far fewer crevices for red mite to hide in. Since about 2000 a few poultry houses have come on the market made of plastic and other unconventional (in this context) materials. Their main advantage is washability, but those seen so far seemed expensive compared to others of similar size in wood/plywood, plus, in the longer term, they are likely to be irreparable when they have been in use for a few years. Plastic, when exposed to sunlight for some years, often goes very brittle; but the materials used for these houses have probably been tested for weather resistance. Those thinking of buying should obtain as many catalogues as possible, and inspect actual specimens (at an agricultural show perhaps?) before committing themselves.

Triangular cross-sectioned arks exist in more variations of size and design than one might imagine considering they all share a common overall shape. At the time of writing, two UK manufacturers were producing arks in which the house part is a tunnel-like arrangement along the top, which the author considers dark, stuffy and cramped. These arks would be particularly disastrous for breeds with large tails. Of the more conventional types, with the house at one end, choose a design with some openings to give light and air to the house part. Your birds will need some wind and rain protection on the run part, which may be part of the design (in wood) or added on by the purchaser – in the form of plastic sheeting over one side perhaps.

A selection of small houses and runs, including triangular cross-section arks, for rearing young stock or housing selected breeding trios of adult bantams.

House and run units with a raised house part, to give extra run space under the house, are available, and excellent if expensive. Some are intended to be static, perhaps placed between a garden path and fence; others are intended to be moved every day or so, like arks. These would be best used in places fairly sheltered from the wind, and potential buyers should check them for overall weight – they may be too heavy for daily moving. There is also one static type (Smiths Sectional Buildings Ltd, 'Mackworth') in which the entire house and covered run unit is raised up on legs. This would be an excellent choice for anyone who has difficulty in getting down on their knees to attend to their birds.

Static houses, intended for use with traditionally fenced grassed runs, also come in many sizes and designs. Your chickens will be shut in for many hours during long winter nights, so imagine yourself in their position when inspecting different types. A design with a wire netting covered window will be brighter and airier for your birds. Your birds may fly onto the roof of these houses, many are less than 4 feet (120cm) high, and from this 'launching pad', fly over their run fencing. If the house is in the centre of a large run they may not do so, or if the run is fairly small, consider netting over the top of at least the part of the run where they may make an escape attempt.

— 5 —
Feeding

Old poultry books had long feeding chapters, including recipes for home-made meal mixtures, but today's poultry keepers use commercially formulated chick, grower and layer meal, pellets and crumbs. As pure breeds do not grow as fast or lay as many eggs as the hybrids that these products are designed for, many hobbyists feed some whole grain mixtures as well. Wild jungle fowl, the ancestors of domestic chickens, are omnivorous birds, eating insects, worms and anything else they can catch as well as seeds, berries, grass and so on. Therefore mixed grain alone will not do – it does not contain enough protein or other nutrients. Traditional farmyard poultry flocks may just have been given grain, and probably not much of that, but they could forage in the fields and orchards to mimic their wild ancestors' environment. Most ancient breeds, such as Friesians and Hamburghs, are quite small, so they did not need to find much food anyway.

It is not unusual for commercial egg producers to have well over 100,000 birds, some have a million or more. They also rear replacement birds, buying them as day-old chicks from the hybrid breeding companies. When birds are kept in these numbers, small variations in food consumption, growth rates and egg production levels per bird add up to major effects to the profitability of the enterprise. Tiny variations are even more important to producers of the hundreds of millions of broiler chickens reared annually around the world.

The scientists who work for the feed (it's a tradition of the industry to use 'feed' as a noun, not 'food') companies, plus those at agricultural colleges and similar establishments, have studied the nutritional requirements of all types of poultry in minute detail. Their findings have been used by mill managers to set the parameters of each compound formulation. The list of ingredients that can be found attached to bags of feed do not give exact percentages because they vary slightly according to changes in prices of raw materials. The computer programs used can give the same end product (in terms of percentage of protein, and so on), within pre-set limits, with different combinations of ingredients. Hobbyist poultry keepers can rest assured that the bags of feed they buy will be safe and far better than they could make themselves. All sectors of agriculture and food manufacturing continually make every effort to ensure that nothing like the BSE crisis ever happens again.

Chick crumbs, the normal type intended for layer hybrid chicks rather than broilers, is used from day-old to eight weeks. As pure breeds are slower to reach the equivalent stage of growth it is best to keep them on chick crumbs for at least twelve weeks. Many pure breeds are from inbred strains that are less efficient at absorbing nutrients, so at this stage do not give any grain. The next diet, growers' meal or pellets, is used commercially from eight to twenty weeks. For pure breeds this is changed to twelve weeks until whatever age they are when their comb growth indicates they might be about to start laying. Mixed grain can be introduced, initially in small amounts, from about fifteen weeks. Those fanciers who buy wheat cheaply from local farmers will introduce it earlier and in greater quantities than those who buy all their feed from animal feed retailers, where there is not much difference between the prices of mixed maize and pellets.

The remainder of this chapter attempts to answer some common questions about poultry nutrition and feeding, and highlights some special cases.

Drugs and 'additives' in commercially manufactured feeds

Some companies produce 'organic' rations with none of the drugs and additives that are included in conventional rations. If you have strong opinions on these matters then follow them, for adult birds at least. Conventional chick crumbs and growers' meal/pellets include drugs to prevent (or at least reduce the effects of) coccidiosis, a protozoal disease affecting the intestine walls. Organic rations (without these drugs) are available, but anyone who has experienced a batch of youngsters sicken and die with this horrible disease is not likely to use them. Free-range birds are more susceptible to coccidiosis than those kept in (thoroughly cleaned) houses because coccidia can survive for long periods as spores. You can disinfect the inside of a chicken house, but you cannot disinfect an outside run.

Feeding males

Organic/non-coccidiosis preventative growers meal/pellets is an excellent food for adult males. They do not need the coccidiosis drugs once adult, neither do they need the added calcium in layers' rations for hens to make into eggshells. If mixed grain is being used as well as layers' meal/pellets for breeding groups, males will probably self-regulate by eating a higher proportion of grain as they can be upset by the calcium. This can lead to protein deficiency, which is probably why males often lose condition during the breeding season. Well organized hobbyists, who probably keep a lot more birds than most beginners, have several males of each variety that are alternated with the groups of hens. They are usually kept in individual pens on their 'week off', when they can be fed on a special mix of grain and non-additive growers' ration to restore condition for their next week's 'work'. The integrity of strains is maintained by using two brothers in this system.

Crumbs, meal or pellets?

Ground cereals of various types, soya bean meal and other ingredients are mixed in to produce each type of animal feed made at a mill. Many of these are sold as meal compacted into pellets as customers will have differing ideas about which is best. Commercial laying flocks kept in battery cages or 'barn' systems are confined and are likely to get bored, which can lead to fighting, sometimes even cannibalism. They are usually fed on dry meal as it takes them a long time to eat enough, thereby giving them something to do. Owners of commercially free-range layer flocks may vary, some using meal for the same reasons. Even free-range hens can get bored and start pecking each other. Others choose pellets because they are more concerned about the wastage often associated with meal feeding, the hens flick it out of the troughs and then leave it. If they flick pellets out, they will still eat them from the ground. As hobbyists keep their birds in much smaller groups than commercial egg producers, and even show birds kept inside have a lot more house space per bird than commercial layers, boredom and consequent fighting is less of a problem, so pellets are preferred by most.

Chick crumbs are essentially pellets cut so short that they almost, but not quite, disintegrate back to meal. They are preferable to meal because the pelleting and crumbling process permanently mixes all the ingredients so the chicks cannot pick out all the pretty yellow fragments of maize, an essential but low-protein ingredient. This is the chicken equivalent of small children who would eat nothing by ice cream if they were allowed to.

Pellets can be made in various sizes, and some brands of growers' and layers' pellets intended for normal chickens may be too large for tiny bantams. You may need to change brands.

Food consumption and environmental temperature

Just like humans, poultry eat more when they are cold than when they are hot. Their protein needs are constant, they are changing their intake to adjust their energy (calorie) needs. The traditional way of allowing poultry to self-regulate their needs is to feed pellets (higher protein) in the morning feed and mixed grain in the afternoon. They will eat a lot more grain in winter as the whole grains, being relatively slow to digest, will keep them warm during long, cold, winter nights. In very hot weather it may be necessary to cut out grain completely, to avoid protein deficiencies when they automatically reduce their feed intake.

Bullying and trough space

Chickens, even cute little bantams, can be nasty-natured thugs with each other. The smallest or timid birds may not get enough to eat because they are driven away from food troughs by the dominant birds. It is obviously essential to provide enough troughs/bowls to enable all birds to feed simultaneously. If you have any doubts, throw a handful or two of feed on the floor of the house away from the trough for the 'victims' to eat in peace. This can become a habit with a few birds, who begin to expect their dinner to be served in 'their special place'. Well, they are our pets. If you are intending to keep several breeds, this is a good reason to choose a selection of approximately similar-sized types. Remember, very large but docile Cochins or Orpingtons may be bullied by smaller, but more aggressive breeds.

Food consumption and disease

Birds with intestinal worms will greedily eat more than usual, and still lose weight and condition. Seek veterinary advice or, where you are able to do so, buy a suitable worming treatment from your animal feed retailer. With most other diseases, affected birds eat less than normal, which further reduces their chance of recovery. They have to be tempted to eat by moistening their pellets with a little hot water. Only dampen and give as much as they are likely to eat in a few hours, because damp pellets will rapidly deteriorate.

Grit

There two types of grit, insoluble flint grit that remains in the birds' gizzards to grind grain for it to be easily digested, and oystershell grit, which is soluble, to be absorbed and passed to the oviduct wall to make eggshells. Layers' meals and pellets contain ground limestone to do this, so oystershell grit is not always necessary; however, it does seem to help if hens are laying eggs with thin, porous shells. Flint grit is essential for birds being fed on whole grain that are kept inside. Birds with access to a fairly large outside run will often find enough small stones themselves. Grit is not necessary for chicks fed on chick crumbs.

Water

Poultry, like all other livestock, needs unlimited access to clean water. Empty, clean and refill all water containers daily.

Eggs are mainly composed of water, so laying birds will need more drinking water than non-layers. Like us, all poultry will drink more in hot weather than cold. For both reasons, it may be necessary to provide more or larger water containers during summer.

A wide range of containers is used for drinking water, among the most popular being the fairly cheap plastic types that hold the water in by partial vacuum, releasing a little at a time to the bottom trough part. In very cold weather, when water freezes, swells, and often splits these drinkers, many poultry keepers temporarily switch to ice cream tubs and other 'disposables'.

— 6 —
Incubation and Chick Rearing

Eggs for Incubation

Eggshells, internal membranes and albumen have natural defence mechanisms to protect embryos against bacteria and moulds, but these cannot protect them in poor conditions. Nests must be dark and inviting, so the chickens use them, and nest litter regularly replaced. Eggs should be collected as often as possible, certainly not left overnight in early spring when temperatures might fall below freezing. Once frozen, the embryos will have been destroyed. Using a pencil, write the date and identification code (for breed, group and so on) on the eggshell as you pick each egg up. Do not rely on your memory to do it later, especially if you have several breeding pens laying similar eggs. Fanciers usually have their own code of initials and numbers for this. Eggs can be stored at cool room temperature, not your fridge, for up to twelve days before significant numbers of the embryos cease to be viable.

Assuming you have more eggs than you are able to hatch, carefully select the best ones for incubation. Look for classic egg shape (not long and thin or almost round), shell quality (smooth and shiny, not rough and porous), shell colour (especially brown- and blue-egg breeds), and give preference for fairly large (but not double-yolked) eggs for large fowl, and fairly small eggs for bantams (many bantam breeds are oversized). Sometimes the hens that you are really desperate to breed from (a show winner or very rare breed) lay eggs that fail in one or more of these respects, in which case you will just have to try them, and hope for the best.

Broodies

Beginners should remember that not all breeds go broody and make good mothers. Although breeds that seldom go broody, Leghorn chickens, for example, sometimes do so, they hardly ever finish the job, abandoning their eggs long before they are due to hatch. Groups of more reliable breeds should be given as many inviting nests as there is space for in their house during the breeding season, so they do not disturb each other when laying. Individual plastic drum or cardboard box nests are best for chickens and bantams as each hen, once it has settled down on some dummy eggs for a few days, can be moved to an individual pen (for example, show training cage) in its nest, to complete the job in peace. Sitters of all species usually come off their nest once a day, usually when you do the regular morning feed, to eat, drink and defecate. Hens in nests, in show training cages, must have individual food and water pots. They do not need to be shut in their nests, except for the first night when you moved them into the cage from their original house.

As eggs for hatching are being collected daily, two dummy eggs should be left in each nest throughout the breeding season if you wish to encourage hens and bantams to go broody. Before a hen is moved in her nest (or moved to a fresh nest from houses with built-in nest boxes), she should be allowed to really settle. The first evening you see a hen on a nest instead of her perch, give her two or three more dummy eggs. After she has been moved, do not replace the dummy eggs with the real ones she is to hatch for a day or two. Do the egg swapping in the evening, when she is ready to sleep anyway. Do not put more eggs under a hen than she can cover properly, especially early in spring when nights can be very cold. Typical part-Silkie crossbreds will only be able to hatch eight large eggs.

Write and pin up a card with details of the eggs under each broody, date started and date due by each cage, especially if you have several broodies, all of which started on different days. Shut each hen in her nest the evening before the eggs are due to hatch so that the first chicks to hatch cannot accidentally fall out of the nest before all its brothers and sisters have hatched. Some batches of chicks all hatch within a few hours, others are slower. In the latter case, if the hen shows signs of becoming agitated, wanting to take her brood out of the nest to feed, as her jungle fowl ancestors would have done, transfer any unhatched eggs showing signs of life (cheeping) to an incubator. If the last chicks hatch, you will be able to put them back with the hen.

Chick Rearing with Broody Hens

Paintings of idyllic farmyard scenes may show hens with chicks

The hen and chicks running outside may look idyllic, and the few chicks that avoid getting lost or taken by rats, hawks or other predators may be very fit and healthy, but the family housed inside are much safer at this age. When ready to come away from the broody, at about two months of age, two or more groups of similar-sized youngsters can be amalgamated and given a house with a secure outside run until they are big enough to be safe in more 'free-range' conditions.

131

scratching about outside but, in the real world, very few of them survived the hazards of the countryside. Hens and their chicks should be transferred to a clean and safe environment, a fairly large rabbit hutch of traditional wooden construction is ideal. You may find some for sale (cheap) in local paper small-ads. They can be moved on to a larger house after a few weeks, the exact timing usually depending on what other houses are empty, when later broodies are due to hatch and so on. By early summer, hobbyist poultry breeders need two or three times the number of cages, coops and other small houses for sitting hens, hens with chicks and groups of half-grown youngsters than they needed in the winter, when there were only adult birds to accommodate.

Drinkers and food pots for hens and chicks must be low enough for the chicks to use safely, and heavy enough to prevent scratching mother hens accidentally flipping them over, on top of unfortunate chicks.

Which Incubator to Buy?

There are many different models on the market, in a range of sizes, levels of sophistication and prices. Factors to consider when deciding which to buy include:

1. Size. Incubators are available from small, twelve-egg models up to machines that hold several thousand eggs. Remember that some eggs will be infertile, others will be fertile, but still not hatch, and of those that do, half of the chicks will be males. You will need to incubate a lot more eggs than you might think to end the season with the required number of female youngsters. On the other hand, incubator temperature can fluctuate, even with the latest control systems, if they are run much less than half full. Most hobbyists choose incubators between 40 and 200 hen egg capacities. Check how adaptable each model is for holding small bantam or large eggs.
2. Automatic turning? There are still manual turning machines on the market, and they are cheaper than automatic turning machines, but it is a false economy. Even if you are normally at home to turn the eggs the required minimum of three times a day, people forget, have to go out some days and so on. Buy an automatic egg-turning incubator.
3. 'Still Air' or 'Fan-Assisted'? Heat naturally rises, so only small incubators with all the eggs on one level can be set to give the correct level for all eggs without an internal fan. All incubators

with shelves of eggs at several levels must have internal fans to give an even temperature throughout.

4. General Construction and Design. Look for models with a thick outer casing for good insulation properties, both for economic electricity consumption and temperature stability. Also check how easy it is to clean them internally. Remember, it will have to be thoroughly cleaned between each batch of eggs.
5. Does it come with a good, understandable instruction book?
6. Are spare parts likely to be easily and quickly available?

Checking Eggs During Incubation – 'Candling'

Infertile eggs and those containing dead embryos must be removed from incubators or broodies because they can go rotten and 'rob' heat from healthy embryos. After dark, carefully hold each egg over a torch (UK)/flashlight (US), and you can see if anything is growing inside. It can be difficult to see anything inside eggs with dark brown, blue or green shells at any stage, but white to light brown eggs allow enough light through to see what's happening after about eight or nine days of incubation. With experience, you can cut down to the seventh day.

Infertile ('clear') eggs will just show a yellowish yolk. Developing embryos will show as a black spot, and you will also see a network of blood vessels developing just inside the shell, absorbing oxygen from outside and nutrients from the egg contents. This system breaks down, often into a single 'blood ring' with dead embryos (early dead germs or e.d.g.).

Hobbyists, especially those with breeds that are known not to be very fertile, often have two smaller incubators rather than one big one. They start both the same day, and if fertility is as bad as normal, transfer the remaining eggs into one machine, restarting the other with another lot of eggs. If they have more than one hen go broody at the same time, they will swap eggs around under them in the same way.

Some Causes of Infertility and Dead Embryos

1. Inbreeding. Many pure breeds are kept as closed flocks, which can bring inbreeding problems unless quite a lot of birds are kept, with careful record-keeping to minimize very close relations being mated together. There are very good reasons for this policy, so buying in completely unrelated stock can solve one problem, although it might create others.

2. Extreme cold and hot environmental temperatures can affect the general health of your birds, with consequences for their breeding performance. Is your poultry housing designed as well as it could be for where you live?

3. Dirty eggs are less likely to hatch than clean ones, so do not blame the birds for your failings in nest provision, cleaning out, regular egg collection and so on.

4. Preferential Mating. Not all cockerels are as promiscuous as popularly supposed. Some breeds are almost monogamous, forming stable relationships with one or two females and ignoring any others in the breeding pen. Two cockerels, brothers perhaps, can be used with a group of hens, which one hopes will have different favourites, but on alternate days to prevent them fighting.

Rearing Incubator-Hatched Chicks

As a heat lamp is required, you will need a dry and secure building with an electricity supply, a garden shed or part of your garage perhaps. Infrared lamps will be needed for larger groups of chicks, but smaller groups, up to thirty say, will have enough heat and space by using an ordinary 100- or 150-watt bulb over a large box, about 60cm wide, 90cm long and 60cm high. Even if an ordinary light bulb is used, you must buy the heat-resistant holders designed for use with infrared bulbs. These are available from farm supplies retailers. You will also need to buy one of the metal reflectors made to go with them, to direct heat down to the chicks. Temperature is regulated by lowering or raising the lamp, and by changing to smaller-wattage lamps/light bulbs as the chicks grow, so becoming less dependent on heat. Any ordinary light bulbs used must be the screw-fitting type, heat-resistant holders are not made for normal UK bayonet-fitting light bulbs.

There are a range of designs of boxes and cages used for chick rearing, many use large cardboard boxes (TV set size). Try to visit a few local poultry breeders well before you are likely to rear chicks, and copy whichever ideas seemed best for your circumstances. Hygiene is important; this favours cardboard boxes (that are dumped and replaced each season) and permanent chick-rearing pens with washable surfaces, possibly made from melamine board as normally used for kitchens, utility rooms and so on.

As incubator-hatched chicks do not have a mother to show them what is food and what isn't, it is safest to cover the floor of the chick pen with coarse material (for example, an old hessian sack) or a piece of old carpet. This can be covered with wood shavings in the second week, by which time they will be safely eating chick crumbs. As chicks will be pecking around randomly for the first couple of days, sprinkle some chick crumbs all over their pen floor as well as the main supply in whatever shallow pet bowls or other containers you are using. Only use the smallest sizes of drinkers for chicks, they could drown in larger models. Some chicks, especially day-old turkeys, seem very slow to learn, so you may have to gently dip the beaks of a few of them in their water to teach them to drink. Once a couple start, the rest will follow.

Switch on the heat lamp when you first see cracks in the eggs – this gives a day for the rearing pen to warm up before they are ready to come out of the incubator. The chicks will tell you if the temperature is correct: all huddled together right under the lamp – they're too cold; all spread around the edge of the pen – they're too hot.

Lakenvelder chicken by C.S.Th. Van Gink.

— 7 —
Poultry Clubs and Shows

Pure breeds of poultry are now kept as a hobby, with poultry shows being the traditional meeting places for fanciers. Shows are held in many countries, including Australia, Canada, Japan, New Zealand, the USA and all over Europe. Most of these countries have a national club with affiliated local clubs and specialist breed clubs. Some of these clubs also cater for fancy pigeon (not racing pigeon), rabbit and other small livestock-based hobbies.

National Clubs

Many of these have existed for a century or more, such as the American Poultry Association (APA, 1873) and the Poultry Club of Great Britain (PCGB, 1877). It is considered quite an honour to be elected to the governing councils of these organizations, which is sometimes important when difficult decisions have to be made. Club officials need to know they have the respect of the majority of fanciers for some of their functions, which include the following.

- Testing and keeping a register of show judges
- Disciplinary measures against show cheats or other people causing problems.
- Publishing breed standards book.
- Having a final say in accepting any proposed changes to breed standards or new varieties.
- Representing our hobby to government departments (ref. poultry disease control, and so on).
- Administering a leg ringing scheme.
- Organizing a national show.
- Publishing newsletters, yearbooks, and so on.

A breed club stand at a UK show, The Welsummer Club.

Breed Clubs

These are national clubs for breeders of a single breed or group of related breeds. The breeds that have a specialist club are dependent on their popularity in each country. In the UK there is also The Rare Poultry Society (RPS), and in the USA, The Society for the Preservation of Poultry Antiquities (SPPA), both of which cover those breeds that are not kept by enough people for special clubs to be viable.

Some of their functions are specialized versions of the national club functions given above, or are different parts of the same processes. For example, if a historic breed from another country is imported, it will be the RPS or SPPA that translates the relevant breed standard from that breed's country of origin, and then presents it for acceptance by the PCGB or APA.

Breed clubs encourage existing fanciers by awarding extra prizes (certificates, rosettes and so on, not cash) for relevant class winners at shows all over the country, and help beginners to locate stock. They work with the national club to organize judges, prizes and so on for their relevant sections of national shows.

137

A poultry show in the hall at the Bath & West agricultural showground, Shepton Mallet.

Local Poultry Clubs

These cover all breeds, sometimes fancy pigeons, rabbits and so on, as well, and organize local shows, and often run these sections of summer agricultural shows (=US State Fairs) on behalf of the overall event organizers. Many also have regular monthly meetings with guest speakers, but it is not always easy to find people who can simultaneously interest beginners and lifelong exhibitors, which is why you might find some clubs have given up on regular meetings. Some clubs arrange for bulk buying of feed, vaccines and other essentials, or at least enable local poultry keepers to get to know each other in informal groups.

Entering a Show

New poultry keepers who are thinking of entering their first local show will usually have attended at least one show before to see what they are like. They should have noticed that the birds are arranged in classes of breeds, plus, in the UK and some other countries, mixed AOV (Any Other Variety) classes for groups of broadly similar breeds of which only one or two have been entered of each. Most British exhibitors would rather take their chances in a competitive class than be awarded first out of one. Show organizers need some time to collate the birds entered by each person into the classes, and hence cage numbers, so entry forms are sent out (for small shows) about six weeks beforehand, and must be returned to the show secretary at least two weeks in advance. These lead times are much longer for major shows where professionally printed catalogues, listing every one of sometimes 6,000+ entries, must be arranged as well. Some small shows allow entries to egg classes on the day, but not birds.

Some forthcoming shows are listed in poultry magazines, but it is safest to join your local club well before you are likely to start showing to be sure of being on their mailing list. Show forms are in two parts in most countries, three parts in the UK and some other countries. British shows have pre-set lists of breed classes, whereas many other countries' show organizers enter the birds in a standard, computer-based, class format. These administrative differences are related to differences in judging methods and competitive atmosphere, which there is not space enough to explain fully here. The two show forms that are common to all countries are the entry form (that must be correctly filled in and sent back) and the information sheet with details of:

- Closing date for entries, entry fees per bird and per egg entry.
- Date and location of show, including a map if thought necessary.
- Judging start time (all birds to be in their show cage by …).
- Expected finish time.
- Names of the judges. It does not always say which judge is doing which breed because they often give each judge the same (±) number of birds to do, and no one can accurately predict how many of each breed will be entered.
- The main prizes offered, usually a mix of trophies, small cash prizes and practical items, such as bags of pellets donated by a local feed store.
- Local show rules. National clubs set general show rules, so only a few specific to that show are printed. In the UK, with our pre-scheduled classes, there is some variation in how many birds must be entered to avoid birds being moved to AOV classes.

Suffolk and Essex Poultry Club Show, with judge Trevor Thompson checking which class winners will go on to higher awards. At this stage the first prize cards (red) are placed back-to-front so the judges cannot see the owners' names. This is a typical UK winter local show held in a village hall.

The Suffolk and Essex Poultry Club Show is almost over, and the main winners have been moved to 'Champions Row' ready for the presentation of trophies to their proud owners.

140

Poultry section at a summer agricultural show, actually run by the nearest local poultry club.

Entry Forms

1. Each line represents an exhibit, and therefore a cage. If you are entering more than one bird in a class, write the details however many times are necessary.
2. Be sure to fill in all the columns, so the show secretary will know the breed, colour, sex, size (large or bantam) and, for some shows, the age (under a year or over a year) of each bird.

The amalgamating of classes with only one or two entries into AOV classes has already been mentioned, but it can work the other way as well. As a new exhibitor to a small local show your entries might boost the numbers of some breeds that had previously been in AOV classes at this show to enough for the secretary to take them out of AOV and set up a separate breed class. The same might apply to colour varieties within a breed, which, thanks to you, might jump from a single class for all colours and both sexes of a breed, to separate classes for M&F, perhaps also with a separate class for the most popular colour variety. Show Secretaries can only do this if everyone fills up their forms properly.

There are AOV classes for each section (Large Light Breed, Large Heavy Breed, and so on), so you must know which AOV class is the correct one if you are keeping a breed without a pre-set class. Remember, many breeds that are 'rare' in the general sense of the word are not necessarily 'Rare' in the specific PCGB show rules sense.

Egg Showing

With the ever increasing numbers of suburban poultry keepers who are not allowed to keep cockerels, the egg sections of poultry shows have become steadily more popular. They were once a very minor part of shows, and were unique to the UK, but are now becoming a major part of poultry shows in several Continental countries as well.

Classes are provided for a single egg, a plate of three, or a plate of six, in each case divided into large white, large brown, large blue, bantam white and so on. It is surprising, and sometimes frustrating, how many trays of eggs you have to go through to find three (or six) identical eggs of classic egg shape, free of any shell blemishes, to put a winning exhibit together.

The Judges

All judges are also competent exhibitors, although the most successful do not necessarily make the best judges in the same way that the most talented sports stars do not always go on to become the best trainers, team managers or sports administrators. A good judge must have a calm and consistent approach, combined with an encyclopedic knowledge of all breeds. We all have favourite breeds, but that must be mentally put to one side when judging; and we must certainly put aside the fact that the owners of many of the birds we judge are our friends. Truly impartial judges are remembered for the times they give 'Best in Show' to breeds it is widely known they wouldn't accept as a gift.

Would-be judges do not have to acquire the necessary encyclopedic knowledge instantly, the judges' tests administered by the PCGB and other national clubs are in manageable sizes, a few breeds at a time. Most people start with the test that includes the main breed they keep, so in the UK a Leghorn breeder would take the Soft Feather Light Breeds test first. Only a few judges ever take and pass all the judging tests. In this example, our imaginary aspiring judge might go on to pass the Soft Feather Heavy Breed, True Bantam and Egg tests, and never even attempt the Hard Feather, Rare Breeds and Waterfowl tests. As most shows need three or four judges, show organizers do not need all of them to be all-rounders.

8

Show Preparation

Everyone can appreciate that the snow-white birds seen at poultry shows, along with crested, feather-footed and long-tailed breeds must have been expertly prepared to look as magnificent as they, or at least the best of them, do. Apart from a very few talented individuals, very few beginners are likely to succeed with these demanding varieties. This still leaves a lot of breeds that are much easier to prepare for showing, but even these cannot be just caught from their house on the morning of the show and be expected to be an acceptable show exhibit. Judges are regularly disappointed by the birds they find at local shows, especially the summer agricultural shows, which are caked in mud or have significant feather loss, such as several main tail or wing feathers. Sometimes whole classes are so poor that judges refuse to award any prize cards at all, which they are allowed to do under PCGB rules. Birds are often advertised for sale as 'Winner at xxxx Show', or 'Bred from winner at xxxx Show', and the 'poultry establishment' (club officials, judges, and so on) does not want poor-quality specimens to be sold on this basis as it brings pure-bred poultry into disrepute.

This situation can be upsetting and embarrassing for the owners of birds that have been so publicly 'passed' by a judge, and the only way to avoid it happening is for beginners to have a clear idea of judges' expectations before they even enter a show.

1. All birds must actually be the breed they purport to be, and must not have any disqualifying faults. They need not be perfect, even most Show Champions have some minor breed faults. There will probably be a lot of people who are surprised to learn that birds appear in shows that are not even the breed they should be, but it happens. Marans × 'Speckledy Hybrids' look the same as pure Cuckoo Marans to most people, but the judges can tell the difference. Disqualifying faults can either be general (diseases and deformities) or breed specific (wrong type of comb and so on). Breeders seldom, if ever, sell their best birds, but beginners are

most likely to buy the best quality pure breeds available if they contact appropriate breed club secretaries for details of experienced fanciers in their area. Beginners who buy their first birds at poultry auctions or general retail outlets (for example, some garden centres have poultry/pet sections) must do some research before buying.

2. Birds should be reasonably tame and need to have had some 'practice sessions' in a small pen similar to a standard show cage.
3. Birds should be healthy, not be carrying any lice or mites, and be clean.
4. All main wing and tail feathers should be present and unbroken, although judges will make allowances for birds that have not quite finished their annual moult, and for Japanese (Chabo) Bantams (which often have damaged wing feathers because they drag on the ground), Indian Game/Cornish (which have very brittle feathering) and some other 'special cases'. Birds that have had their wing feathers clipped to stop them flying over run fences will be disqualified. Judges will take the attitude that the owner should build higher fences or covered runs. Hens that have lost some head, neck and back feathers by cockerel damage during mating might be OK of the feather loss is minimal, but those with noticeable bare patches will be disqualified.

Show preparation is not just about what you need to do during the few days before a show, but can be thought of as part of every aspect of keeping your birds. The chapters on feeding and housing include several details that illustrate how keeping pure bred poultry healthy, happy and looking as good as possible is different from just keeping hens – for example, the specific perching arrangements needed for some breeds.

Training Birds

As chickens and other domestic poultry are not the most intelligent of creatures, there is only so much you can do. Your aim is for your birds to stand quietly in their show cage when being judged. There are a few breeds where judges are looking for an ideal 'pose', German Langshans and Pekins for example. These might need some extra training sessions, but for most other breeds it is simply a case of ensuring they don't panic when the stranger in a white coat appears. Birds that are very much family pets, eat out of your hand and are regularly stroked and handled, are effectively also show trained as well; they just need some practice sessions in some show cages (or equivalent pens) to complete the process. It helps if you invite visitors to see your flock and wear a variety of clothes for tending them. Birds that only ever see one person, and he/she is always wearing the same old wax coat (or whatever), are likely to panic when faced with lots of strangers at a show.

If possible, have a shed (or part of a larger building) with as many show cages or similar-sized pens as possible for show training. These cages will also be useful for assessing growing stock, displaying birds for sale when potential buyers visit and for other occasions when birds need to be kept individually. Chickens have a limited memory span when it comes to recognizing other chickens, so do not keep birds in these cages for more than a few days each time, or you may have problems trying to put them back in their regular houses.

Judges use extendable lecturers' pointers as 'judging sticks' to move birds around in show cages, so it would be a good idea for you to have one as well in order that your birds don't panic at their first show. If, by chance, you happen to have an old broken radio aerial that was never thrown away, this would do just as well.

Some breeds are naturally tame and confident with people, others have a wilder temperament. Just do the best you can with these, and remember that the judges know all about these breed differences and will make due allowances.

'Is that allowed?'

Birds must be cleaned for showing, and it is considered normal practice to gently remove some broken or incorrectly coloured feathers (for example, Barred breeds often have a few completely black body feathers). Beginners are often not sure how far they are allowed to go before legitimate show preparation becomes faking. Dyeing feathers or artificially colouring ear lobes or shanks and feet are definitely faking, although the Pile colour variety of some breeds have had parts of their plumage bleached by generations of expert exhibitors for well over a century, so this is generally considered the main allowable exception. Read *Exhibition Poultry Keeping* (David Scrivener, The Crowood Press) for more details, plus study the histories of the breeds you decide to keep.

Most allowable removal of feathers is done to small body feathers. No one, including the judge, will notice that any have gone, but there is nothing you can do with main tail and wing feathers. It may well be that a bird you are showing with one or two broken or wrong-coloured wing fathers still wins a prize card if it is better than some others in its class in other respects, so don't lose heart. Those breeds that should have a broad and compact tail of soft feathers (Brahmas, Cochins, Pekins and Wyandottes) will be considerably improved if any long or protruding tail feathers are removed before a show.

Basic Feet and Face Cleaning

There are many varieties that do not normally need a complete pre-show bath if they have been kept in a reasonably clean environment. This is why beginners to showing are advised to start with fairly dark coloured breeds that do not have feathered feet or other extra features. If you have several birds to do, it is probably best to have a bucket of warm water outside to get the worst of the muck and mud off their feet before you move to the kitchen or utility room sink to complete the process. If the show is on a Sunday, do the washing midweek, and keep your birds clean inside in your own show training pens until show day.

Regular exhibitors keep old toothbrushes, towels, face flannels and so on that have been 'retired' from human use for chicken cleaning. An ordinary bar of soap will also be needed, perhaps something stronger, such as industrial hand cleanser (the gritty textured type) for very dirty feet and shanks. Dirt can get under the edges of scales, appearing like dirty fingernails on human hands. It doesn't show on black-legged breeds, but those with white or yellow scales must be gently cleaned, plastic cocktail sticks being the best tool for this job. This is a time-consuming job, although you will get quicker with practice. When you finish cleaning each bird, and have dried it, paper kitchen towels are useful for gently doing their faces, especially near eyes. Give their face, wattles and comb a smear of baby oil, and their shanks and feet a smear of petroleum jelly (for example, Vaseline). You will probably be surprised how much difference this basic feet'n'face washing makes, even to simple dark-coloured breeds like Australorps, when you compare your first washed bird with the other waiting their turn.

A Complete Bath

It would probably be easier if you can arrange to visit an experienced local exhibitor washing their birds, or have him/her come to help you the first time you try to bath a bird, but if it's not possible to arrange this, hopefully this section will help.

Bathing birds is best done in the evening, and once washed and made as dry as possible, first with a towel, then with a hair dryer, your birds should spend the night in show baskets in warm places (by radiators) in your house. It seemed best to mention this final part of bathing first, so you have suitable baskets, pet carriers and so on, ready; perhaps standing on newspaper in carpeted rooms.

Some house-proud beginners might not believe it, but most fanciers do their chicken washing in the kitchen sink if they do not have another sink in a utility room or outbuilding. These birds are, for most of us, as much loved pets as a cat or dog, so we don't have a problem with that. Larger containers, 'antique' galvanized baths perhaps, might be needed, and used in a shed, for very large breeds such as turkeys and so on. Water should be no hotter than blood temperature. Try the traditional elbow test for baby's bath water.

Use dandruff shampoo borrowed from your bathroom or dog shampoo, as these products will remove any lice and mites as well as cleaning the plumage. If you do not have, or forget to buy, either of these, ordinary shampoo or even washing up liquid will do. Before immersing the bird (except its head) in the water, do the feet'n'face cleaning as outlined above, except for the baby oil and petroleum jelly part, which must wait until the bird is completely dry. At all times, gently work in the shampoo from head to tail as even the slightest rubbing the other way will break innumerable feathers. Be sure to open the wings; the flight feathers often need extra gentle scrubbing. When the bird seems as clean as you think it is likely to get, drain the sink and refill with clean water to rinse.

Then gently wrap the bird in a towel and leave it to drip-dry a little, perhaps sitting on your lap. When you start the hair dryer phase of drying the bird, again be sure the air is blowing from head to tail for all parts except the fluff around its vent. Do not try to completely dry the bird with a hair dryer, this would take too long and do too much damage to its plumage. You are just trying to get the bird partially dry before it spends the night by a radiator to fully dry out and fluff up naturally. All bathed birds must, of course, be kept clean and dry until show day. They really need at least two or three days to preen themselves, so replacing lost natural skin oils.

If you also keep some hybrid layers or crossbreeds, it would be a good idea to have a practice session on one of them long before you need to do any potential show birds.

Transporting Show Birds

Beginners have usually visited several shows before actually entering one, so you should have seen the assortment of boxes, baskets and pet carriers everyone else uses. After all the preparation work you have already done, you do not want to have it all ruined by birds fighting in their boxes on the way to the show or having their lovely tail feathers crushed by being in too small a container. New baskets and pet carriers are quite expensive, so look out for some at car boot sales; and there is nothing wrong with using strong cardboard boxes (with added ventilation holes) that you may be able to collect from friends, your workplace or wherever. Aim to have a suitable collection ready so birds can be taken in suitable-sized containers, individually or, if in groups, only three at the maximum, and these must be birds who regularly live together. All containers should have some clean woodshavings for the birds to sit on. In case they make themselves dirty on the way, take some soap, towels and so on with you in case you have to do an emergency cleaning job when you arrive. *See* the Poultry Clubs and Shows chapter for details of how to enter (several weeks before the show).

The Day of The Show

Having cleaned your birds and prepared suitable containers to transport them in, allow plenty of time for the journey so you are not rushed when you arrive, which ideally should be an hour before judging is due to start. Before you start unloading your vehicle, go into the hall (or tent) and collect your 'penning slip' from the organizer's table. Some clubs use the original entry form (or a photocopy of it), with the 'secretary's column' filled in with the cage number for each bird. Find your birds' cages, and then start bringing your birds in. If you find there has been a mistake, a large fowl in the bantam class (or vice-versa) of the same breed for example, find one of the show organizers before losing heart: it is often possible to arrange an alternative cage. Many clubs put up a few spare cages, and some exhibitors may have been unable to bring some of their birds. Bring some cleaning materials (soap, tissues and so on) in case of last minute problems, and the vaseline or baby oil for shanks, feet and combs. It has been normal practice not to give food or water pots to birds until after judging, although this is changing: do not give very much food, and ensure only proper hook-on water pots are used. If a water pot is tipped over it will make a mess, and could ruin the chances of some breeds, especially those with feathered feet and head crests.

Once all the birds are in their correct cages, it's time for a cup of tea and a chat with the other exhibitors. Do not approach the judges until they have finished. Most judges stay for an hour or two after all classes, section winners and show champions have been decided. As the prize cards are first put up all the first prize cards are put up back-to-front – this is done to prevent the judges seeing the exhibitors' names until they have chosen the major award winners. Judges are allowed to withhold awards if, as sometimes happens at smalll shows, all the birds in a class are a very poor lot or have been disqualified for having external parasites. Conversations with judges after judging can be very useful for beginners, particularly those who are trying several breeds and are intending to specialize in only some of them in the future. The advice given may not necessarily reflect awards given on the day; a bird disqualified for have mites may be a good bird, and a winner of a small class may be quite poor compared with those of its breed elsewhere in the country.

White German Langshan bantams by C.S.Th. Van Gink. Note the 'wine glass' outline of the ideal pose, which exhibitors hope their birds will adopt when being judged.

9

Turkeys

Despite their name, wild turkeys originated in the Americas. There are two wild species, the main one, *Meleagridis gallopavo*, from which domestic turkeys are derived, existing in five sub-species. The other species, the Ocellated Turkey (*Meleagridis ocellata*), is becoming rare in parts of Mexico, Guatemala, Belize and Honduras. These are kept by a few zoos, but are rarely seen in private collections. *Meleagridis gallopavo* was domesticated by ancient civilizations in Mexico about 2,000 years ago, when their feathers were valued as much as their flesh. The more settled communities in North America, the Pueblo tribes in the south-west (for example, the Hopi and Navajo), Cherokee and Iroquois in the east also kept turkeys from about AD700. They had already established several colour varieties before Europeans arrived.

All the early European explorers of the Americas, initially the Spanish Conquistadors, saw the potential of the turkey, and took specimens back home on their return voyages. The first turkeys in England were brought over by William Strickland of Boynton, Yorkshire in the 1520s. They were spread over the whole of Europe during the sixteenth and seventeenth centuries. By 1600 they had become a fairly common sight in farmyards all over Europe, on larger farms at least.

Wild turkeys are smaller and more active than domestic turkeys. American farmers in the eighteenth and nineteenth centuries used their moderate-sized, and still very active, domestic turkeys as organic pest controllers. This was especially true on tobacco plantations, where turkeys ate millions of 'tobacco hornworms', a type of moth larva that would destroy crops if unchecked. The American tradition of eating turkey on Thanksgiving Day was no doubt encouraged by these farmers, coming as it did after the (tobacco) harvest, when the turkeys were up to killing size and (apart from breeding stock) were not needed for bug hunting for a few months.

The main objective of selective breeding in turkeys has been to increase their growth rate and eventual size. Since the 1950s this has reached extraordinary levels, with commercial birds having to be artificially inseminated. Modern stags are simply too big to manage it! Exhibition turkeys are rather less well developed, which many people who are concerned about 'progress' in selective breeding will probably welcome. Because the show turkeys are slower-growing, they will have more flavour than commercials, and even the largest of them will look thin when compared to the turkeys in your local supermarket.

When fanciers speak of 'Turkey Breeds', they are effectively talking about colour varieties. Some are larger than others, officially 'Light' and 'Heavy', but there are none of the variations in shape, leg and tail lengths and so on as seen with chickens. Very small 'dwarf' turkeys exist, mostly in research establishments. If they become widely available to hobbyists, and are bred in the full range of colours, they are certain to become very popular pet/show birds. Many would-be suburban poultry breeders are prevented from joining our hobby because they cannot keep crowing cockerels. Turkeys are much quieter, and these dwarf turkeys are small enough to be kept in a normal suburban garden. Although normal sized turkeys are equally quiet, and are not messy like ducks and geese, a breeding flock, plus extra housing for growing stock, would take up more space than most of us have. When kept in small numbers, turkeys often become very tame, so making excellent pets, but anyone thinking of having some should be realistic about the space they will need.

TURKEY COLOUR VARIETIES

Bronze

This is the colour of wild turkeys, although there are some variations between the sub-species. Both sexes are glossy metallic-bronze on most parts, with white barring on the main wing feathers and brown, black and white bands across tail feathers, as seen most clearly on stags when displaying.

Cambridge Bronze A duller version of the above.

Black Winged Bronze A rare variation of Bronze with a pinkish sheen, which accounts for their alternative name, Crimson Dawn. As the name indicates, their main wing feathers are solid black, not barred as on normal bronze turkeys.

Bronze Turkey male.

Narrangansett A beautiful metallic silver-grey variation of the Bronze pattern. They are named after Narragansett Bay, Rhode Island, and were bred long before they were recognized in the first edition (1874) of *The American Standard of Excellence*. They are bred, but are very rare, in the USA, UK, The Netherlands and Germany.

British White (UK) and White Holland (US) These names have been adopted for all non-commercial (that is, non-broad-breasted) white turkeys. They are very rare because most hobbyist turkey keepers prefer the other prettier and more interesting colours. It is to be hoped that a few people continue to keep them so there are some white turkeys in the world that are as unrelated as possible to the broad-breasted commercial strains.

Norfolk Black

Named simply 'Black' in other countries, they have a special place in British history as they were the first colour other than bronze established in large enough numbers to be reognized as a specific breed. As a result of occasional crossing with Bronze turkeys, not all Norfolk Blacks are as black as one would wish. Good, solid black, specimens are very smart; and the less-than-black stags are one of the meatier 'Heritage' turkeys.

Blue-Slate This colour is caused by a gene that dilutes black to a bluish grey, very similar to blue chickens. Like blue chickens, only a small proportion of each season's youngsters will be a nice even blue, without black flecks or bronzy/reddish shading to spoil the effect. As with Blacks, breed as many as you can, and expect to eat a lot of turkeys!

Buff and Bourbon Red

Buffs are an attractive cinnamon shade, darker than buff chickens; and Bourbon Reds are a darker brownish red shade with black edgings on stags. Both are fairly rare in the UK, with some Buff × Bourbon Reds around. Anyone thinking of trying either of these colours should closely study the *Standards* and consult some experts before buying. The feathers of both of these varieties are light, almost white, near to the skin, so feather stubs do not show on plucked birds.

Cröllwitzer/Royal Palm/Ronquières

These are all white with (slightly different) black markings, and being very pretty are becoming very popular among hobbyist turkey keepers. Again, consult some experts to sort out which is which.

Auburn and Silver Auburn

These are two brown varieties that retain the pattern and metallic gloss of Bronze and Narrangansetts. It's a shame they are very, very rare.

Nebraskan Spotted and Harvey Spotted

Both are white turkeys with irregular black (Nebraskan) or reddish brown (Harvey) spots, and both are very rare. Some people will think them very pretty, but exhibition poultry keepers who are used to specific plumage patrterns may not like their random spotting.

Cröllwitzer Turkey male.

TURKEY HOUSING

Once they are past the chick ('poult' in turkeys) stage, they are hardy birds. They need a lot of ventilation, but not a howling gale. For most of the twentieth century turkeys have often been kept in simple 'pole barns', not much more than a corrugated iron roof on wooden posts. The side(s) that face north and/or the prevailing wind on the site is solid (wood/corrugated iron/corrugated plastic in various combinations). The remaining side(s) are usually solid up to the turkey's head height, with wire netting or weldmesh above. Assuming one has the space, make a long narrow shed divided into pens for separate breeding or rearing groups, each pen about 3 or 4 metres square.

Turkeys are large birds, so need wide perches, not too high, and well away from the house walls. Perches should be at about the turkey's head height, and about 7.5 to 10cm wide. If perches are too close to the wall the turkeys will break their tail feathers. Do not allow young turkeys on perches, their breast bones will be deformed if you do. Give youngsters some bales of straw to sleep on at this stage – they will enjoy jumping on and off the bales during the day as well.

There have been quite a lot of 'ideal' designs for nest boxes for turkeys, and we all know that hobbyist poultry keepers are masters of the art of recycling. Whether nest boxes are purpose-made, or old packing cases, redundant dog kennels or whatever, size is critical. Each box should be large enough for one hen to sit comfortably, preferably without breaking tail feathers. Turkey hens will prefer the darkest nest boxes, usually those in the corners, and valuable hatching eggs might get broken if two or more hens try to squeeze into the favourite nests. Sometimes the stag will try to sit in on the act as well.

Turkeys keep much fitter, healthier and more fertile if they have access to a large outside run, not a squalid mud patch. Run fencing should be high enough to keep your turkeys in and foxes out, and with the foxes (and badgers) in mind, they must be secure around the base, with suitable measures taken to ensure predators cannot dig their way in. If a long shed (divided into pens) is built, grass will last longer if there are fewer, larger, outside runs, perhaps one outside run for two or three shed pens, and the turkeys let out on a rota basis. Of course, if you have the space and suitable layout to give a large outside run for each house pen this is better – but in the real world, few people are that lucky.

TURKEY BREEDING

No doubt most turkey keepers eat some of their eggs, but turkeys are essentially table birds, and it is normal practice to treat every egg as if it were going to be incubated, whether or not this is actually going to happen. Turkey hens can lay eighty or more eggs in their first year, but they won't if you leave their eggs in the nest and they go broody as soon as they've laid a dozen or so. It is standard practice to remove eggs to begin with, hatching them in an incubator or under a large broody chicken. The turkey hens can be allowed to hatch their own later in the season.

One key item of equipment essential for turkey breeding that is not used on any other type of poultry is the 'turkey saddle'. They are canvas pads, held in place by straps that fit under the hens' wings ('armpit' is not really an applicable term for a turkey), and are needed because turkey stags, being much heavier than the hens, can severely injure a hen's back during mating. Turkey Club UK will advise on sources of turkey saddles, so don't worry about having to make them yourself. It is difficult to be definite about how many hens a stag can keep fertile, lighter-weight birds can be very vigorous, whereas some heavy-weights have trouble managing to successfully mate at all, although not for the want of trying.

Incubator-hatched turkey poults are reared under heat lamps in the same way as chicks, but must have proper Turkey Starter Crumbs – ordinary Chick Crumbs will not do. Turkeys need more protein and the anti-Blackhead (a disease of turkeys) supplements included. Similar considerations apply to the nutrition of turkeys of all ages, they are much more demanding than chickens. Be aware that different rations are fed to turkeys being fattened for the table, for their last weeks at least, from those of birds that are to be kept for future breeding. This should not be too difficult for a well organized turkey keeper with enough housing for all likely eventualities. Turkey stags are already quite large before they need to go on fattening pellets, and if there are a dozen or so to be fattened, they can be kept in a separate pen.

American Mammoth Bronze cock, Cambridge Bronze hen, Buff hen and White cock by J.W. Ludlow. Originally a free gift with Feathered World *magazine, 6 December 1912.*

— 10 —
Health and Disease

Novice poultry keepers often worry too much about serious poultry diseases and not enough about mundane problems like lice, mite, including scaly leg mite, and worms. Your birds are only in danger of catching one of the major diseases when an epidemic is in progress, and the news media will be keeping us all informed when that happens.

Serious diseases need the services of a vet to diagnose and treat them. The symptoms of a lot of diseases are very similar – one pale-faced, huddled, fluffed-up, sick chicken looks much like another, even though they may have different diseases. Even your vet will often rely on post-mortem examinations or blood sample testing to confirm many cases. Relatively few vets are really expert on poultry diseases or have relevant drugs in stock. Ask other poultry keepers in your area which one to use in case you ever need one.

If a vet is needed it is usual to take a few typical sick birds to the surgery for examination, as 'house calls' are expensive, and the vet will not need to see the whole flock if they all have the same disease. This does not apply in epidemic situations, when poultry must not be moved.

A lot of the content in other chapters on housing, feeding and general care is effectively also a valuable part of disease prevention. Really healthy birds are more able to fight off infections. Hobbyist poultry keepers are obviously not normally going to have the level of biosecurity arrangements used in the poultry industry, such as disinfectant footbaths, special clothing and very few visitors. If there is an epidemic of a serious disease they should introduce as many of these precautions as are feasible in a domestic situation.

There are a few aspects of poultry care that are not really to do with diseases, but this is probably the best chapter to discuss them.

Moulting

Adult birds drop their old feathers and grow new ones every year in the late summer and autumn. This can be alarming to some novice poultry keepers as hens stop laying and their combs shrink and look pale, almost greyish. A beginner could easily mistake normal changes at moulting time for a disease. The physiological demands of moulting can certainly result in the death of a few birds, but in two or three months' time the majority of your flock will be back to normal, including their proper-sized, healthy-looking red combs. The moulting season is a good time for an intensive session of cleaning out and spraying against lice and mites as they will probably be losing some of these parasites with their old feathers anyway.

Wing Clipping

Chickens that persistently fly over their run fencing can be curtailed by clipping (with a strong pair of scissors or garden shears) the large primary feathers (except the outer two) of one wing only. This throws them off balance when they try to fly. Birds with clipped wing feathers cannot be entered in poultry shows, so exhibitors will have to make their runs escape-proof. Clipped birds may need doing again after a moult, but after a year of not being able to escape few birds are intelligent enough to realize the potential of their nice new wing feathers.

Claw Care

Claws mainly need to be checked on very young chicks and then again on much older birds. If their floor litter is damp and dirty, lumps of faeces can form and harden on their claws, which in very bad cases can result in the claw and even the end part of the toe dying and falling off. Check your chicks' feet regularly and very carefully remove any such lumps. Nail clippers are the best tool for this job. It would be best if you can ask an experienced poultry keeper to show you how to do this without injuring the chicks the first time you have this problem.

The claws on older birds sometimes get very overgrown, even curling round. They should be cut back to a normal length. If you hold the claw up to the light you will be able to see how far blood vessels in the claw extend, then cut just beyond them. Use nail clippers to do this on smaller breeds, you may need garden shears or wire cutters for larger types.

Beak Trimming

Occasionally a bird will have either a crossed beak or a grossly over-grown upper beak. This can affect its ability to eat, and any affected birds cannot be entered in poultry shows. It is quite simple, although naturally requires great care, to improve such beaks with nail clippers. Badly crossed beaks may be the result of a deformed skull, in which case it is best to kill the bird.

Frozen Comb

Breeds with very large single combs can suffer from frost-bitten tips in very cold winters. The first sign is blackening of the tips of the comb. Help the bird retain its body heat by a generous coating of petroleum jelly (for example, Vaseline®™) on its comb. For the duration of the severe weather, move any affected birds to a warmer house, or make their existing house warmer by covering most (but not all) of any open (wire mesh) parts with plastic sheeting.

Egg Eating

Once a hen has discovered that the contents of an egg are tasty, and the other hens in the group often follow the first culprit's lead, this vice can be difficult to stop. It often starts when an egg is accidentally broken, so prevention is better than cure. You should minimize the chances of eggs being broken at all. Eggs laid on the floor of their house instead of in a nest box are most likely to be broken, so ensure there are enough nest boxes for each group of hens, and that nest litter is regularly cleaned out and replaced. Hens will avoid using nests that are infested with red mites.

If a group of hens start egg eating, a move to a new house with a grassy run sometimes helps to stop them by giving them an interesting new environment to occupy their minds. If you do not have a spare house (few fanciers do), simply swap houses with another group. Various forms of 'aversion therapy' have been tried to put hens off egg eating, such as providing dummy eggs that they eventually get bored with pecking at.

External Parasites

There are five main types of deal with: Lice, Northern Mite, Red Mite, Depluming Mite and Scaly Leg Mite. The first are easily visible on the birds, and are mostly found on the skin around the vent. Red Mite can be seen on the skin on all parts of the body at night, and hiding in cracks and crevices in the house, mainly on or near perches and nest boxes, during the day. The last two are too small to be seen with the naked eye, but the damage they do is all too visible. Depluming Mite strips feathers, usually concentrating on neck feathers, down to bare quills. Scaly Leg Mite burrows under the scales of their shanks and feet, creating unslightly and painful crusty deposits. Northern Mite and Red Mite are blood suckers, and bad infestations can kill birds. Before it gets quite that bad, hens will stop laying and cocks will stop mating.

There are several sprays and powders on the market to kill these pests, some intended to be sprayed directly on birds, others for spraying houses, perches and nests. The latter type are too strong for use on birds, and give off strong fumes, so treat houses during the day when the birds are outside.

Scaly Leg Mite is more difficult to treat because whichever sprays or creams are used, they must be applied several times over a month or more. Benzyl Benzoate cream has become a popular treatment in recent years. It can be ordered from most local pharmacists, and is mainly used for a variety of skin conditions on humans, dogs, horses and other animals. Breeds with feathered legs and feet are most susceptible as the feather follicles provide a relatively easy access point for the mites. Do not confuse Scaly Leg Mite infestation with the naturally coarser scales of older birds.

Internal Parasites – Worms

There are several types of worms that affect poultry, all infesting the intestinal tract except for gapeworm, which infests the throat and lungs. Each has a slightly different life-cycle, but in general worm eggs are passed out (in droppings or, in gapeworm, coughed up) and survive outside for a considerable time before they are picked up by another bird. Some types of worm have intermediate hosts, such as earthworms and slugs, increasing the chances of them being eaten by another bird. Outside runs that have become reduced to bare earth by prolonged heavy use are most likely to contain large numbers of worm eggs. Even if your birds did not have any worms when you bought them, worms can be introduced to poultry runs by visiting wild birds.

Gapeworm (*Syngamus trachea*) causes birds to gasp for breath, often with a characteristic neck-stretching motion. However, some other respiratory diseases, many of which can kill an entire flock, give similar symptoms. Consult a vet for a correct diagnosis and treatment.

The other worms all affect parts of the digestive tract, often causing loss of weight and condition despite birds eating as much (or more) food as normal. Yellowish diarrhoea will be seen in the houses and runs, although this can also be caused by protein deficiency, a sudden change in diet or other food-related problems. The worms are: large roundworms (Ascaridia galli), hair worms (*Capillaria obsignata, Capillaria caudiflata, Capillaria contorta* and others), tapeworms (*Davainea proglottina*) and gizzard worms (*Amidostomum anseris* – only affects geese).

Many poultry keepers dose their entire flock once or twice a year to 'clear out' any worms that may be present. You will probably need to go to a vet to obtain a suirable wormer, Flubenvet being the main brand in use at time of writing, although (subject to any future changes in regulations) it may be possible to buy suitable wormers at some agricultural supplies retailers. Regular cleaning out of houses and rotational use of outside runs will help to reduce the numbers of worm eggs that your birds might pick up.

Blackhead and Coccidiosis

These are protozoal diseases that sometimes break out despite commercial rations for young turkeys and chickens having drugs to prevent them. Blackhead (*Histomanis meleagridis*) only affects turkeys, although chickens can act as carriers of the disease. The main symptoms are yellowish diarrhoea and general weakness, with drooping head, wings and tail being noticeable. There may be some darkening of head skin, but this disease's name is really a misnomer. Coccidiosis is caused by a number of *Eimeria* species, *E. tenella* being one of the most deadly. Each species concentrates on a different part of the intestine walls, and each is quite specific about the age of the birds it affects. Adult birds do not normally suffer from Coccidiosis at all. Rabbits also suffer from Coccidiosis, but different types. The damage done by this organism to the intestinal walls of its victims cause weakness, weight loss, and frequently death. Blood can often be seen in their watery droppings. Blackhead and Coccidia eggs can, like worm eggs, survive for long periods in the ground, which is why young growers are often much healthier being raised indoors on nice clean wood shavings than they are (in the popularly assumed healthier) outside. Heat-lamp reared chicks and turkey poults will be kept inside anyway, and it is essential that when they are eventually old enough to go out, it is on to ground that has not been used for any other poultry for (at least) several months.

In clean, controlled conditions the preventative drugs in chick/turkey crumbs/pellets will usually be effective, but hobbyists' housing and general arrangements are not as 'biosecure' as those of the poultry industry, so outbreaks do occur. Consult a vet at the first signs of symptoms for the stronger drugs necessary to save the lives of as many of your young birds as possible. Some people have strong views about 'additives', and chick crumbs without these preventative drugs are available, but apart from use for ducklings and goslings (where the drugs can be harmful and the threat is minimal) I certainly do not advise them.

MAJOR DISEASES AND VACCINES

Most vaccines come in 1,000 dose packs as they are manufactured for commercial hatcheries and farms. Once each pack is opened (often a bottle of diluent has to be mixed with a freeze-dried block of vaccine in a second bottle) it has to be used within a very short time, usually a few hours. Most hobbyists have very small groups of each age, so do not vaccinate their birds at all. Some would not vaccinate even if small dose packs were available, preferring to rely on natural resistance. Of course some fanciers have large collections and run quite big incubators, so for them vaccination is feasible. Most of the vaccines are cheap enough for it to be worth buying a 1,000 dose bottle if you have 100+ chicks in a batch.

Silver spangled Hamburghs by C.S.Th. Van Gink.

Glossary

AOC Any Other Colour classes at UK poultry shows. Popular breeds have several classes in show schedules, some for the main colours, the rarer colours going in AOC classes.

AOV Any Other Variety classes at UK poultry shows. Similar to the above, but for rarer breeds.

Autosexing Breed A group of breeds in which male chicks are lighter-coloured than females.

Bantam General term for miniature chickens in English-speaking countries. In Germany, Bantam is the name of the (English language) Rosecomb bantam breed, the German general term being Zwerg-huhner (dwarf chickens).

Barred Plumage pattern, black and white stripes across feathers. **Cuckoo Barred** is a broader, fuzzier version of the same pattern.

Beard, Beard and Muff, Muff Feather formations under the beak of some breeds, replacing the wattles of most other breeds. The choice of term used is traditional for each relevant breed.

Beetle Brows Prominent 'eyebrows', formed by a combination of unusual skull formation and thick feathering required on some breeds – for example, Brahmas and Malays.

Birchen or Birchen Grey A mostly black plumage pattern with white breast lacing, neck hackles and male saddle hackles.

Black-Red/Partridge The plumage of wild Red Junglefowl and several domestic chicken breeds. *See* photos of Gold Partridge Dutch male and Partridge Modern Game.

Black-Red/Wheaten   Males of this plumage pattern are similar to the above, but the females are delicate cream to fawn shades with some black neck, wing and tail markings.

Blue-Red   Variations of either of the two patterns above, but with all black parts replaced by bluish grey.

Boule   A sweptback feather formation on the neck feathers of Barbu d'Anvers, Barbu d'Uccles and Orloffs.

Brassiness   Yellowish shade on white or lavender plumage caused by prolonged exposure to bright sunlight. A show fault. Prevented by providing shaded runs for these colour varieties.

Breed   Breeds are defined by their body shape, tail formation, leg length and so on. Many breeds exist in two size versions (large and bantam), and several colour varieties.

Carriage   The ideal standing position for a bird at a show. This varies according to breed, some required to stand upright (for example, Modern Game), others, more sedately (for example, Sussex should stand with a horizontal back).

Clean-Legged   No feathers growing on shanks or feet; the opposite of feather-legged.

Cock   A male bird after its adult moult, about eighteen months old.

Cockerel   A male bird younger than a cock.

Cock-Breeder or Cockerel-Breeder   *See* Double mating.

Columbian   Plumage pattern with black neck striping, wing markings and tail over a white ground colour. Called 'Light' on Brahmas and Sussex, and 'Ermine' on Faverolles.

Comb   Fleshy structure on a fowl's head. There are several types, listed separately.

Crest   Feathery structure on a fowl's head, the size and shape varying according to breed.

Crow-Headed A weak skull with a long thin beak, usually associated with poor general growth.

Cull and Culling Sub-standard birds and their removal from a flock. These can range from unhealthy birds to be killed, to birds (in experts' flocks) with minor plumage pattern faults that could be sold with a clear conscience.

Cup Comb A crown-like comb seen on Sicilian Buttercups and few other very rare breeds.

Cushion Thick plumage on the back of birds, a desirable feature on breeds that should have a rounded body shape (*see* photo of Partridge Cochin female), a serious fault on breeds that should have a slim and elegant outline.

Cushion Comb Compact comb type required on Silkies.

Double Laced Plumage pattern of Barnevelders and Dark Indian Game(UK)/Dark Cornish(US).

Double Mating Separate Cock-breeder and Pullet-breeder strains are needed to produce good show birds of some varieties. *It does not mean* that a pullet-breeder cock will only breed female chicks, or that a cock-breeder hen will only lay eggs containing male embryos. *See* the Double Mating chapter of *Exhibition Poultry Keeping* (David Scrivener, The Crowood Press) for a full explanation.

Dual Purpose In the days before hybrid layers and broilers, when pure breeds were kept on general farms, Rhode Island Reds, Sussex and some other breeds were, by the standards of their time, regarded as good layers and table breeds.

Duck-Footed A serious show fault in which the hind toes of a chicken or bantam are around the side of the feet, instead of pointing to the rear.

Duckwing   Plumage colour variety. Silver version of the Black-red/Partridge pattern in which all red, orange and brown parts are replaced by grey or white, except for the salmon breast of Partridge females, which becomes a pinkish shade on Duckwing females. *See* photos of Silver Kraienköppe. Gold Duckwing variety is halfway between Partridge and Silver Duckwing.

Ear Lobes   Oval patch of skin on the side of a fowl's head, below the real ear, a small feather-covered hole. In most cases, white-lobed breeds lay white-shelled eggs and red-lobed breeds lay tinted or brown eggs. White lobes need extra care to keep free of blemishes.

Exhibition Type and Utility Type   Poultry shows were once closely tied to poultry farming, these two activities gradually going their separate ways 1920–40. During this period there were obviously different exhibition and utility types of some breeds. Few utility strains still exist.

Fancier   A person who breeds and shows small livestock. **The Fancy** is a generic term for the hobbies of cage bird, cavy, fancy pigeon, poultry and rabbit keeping and showing.

Feather-Legged   Feathers growing from the toes and shanks (the scaly part of the leg).

Fifth Toe   An extra hind toe that grows above the normal toe (upwards) on a few breeds: Dorking, Faverolles, Houdan, Lincolnshire Buff, Silkie, Sultan.

Foxy   A plumage colour show fault on some varieties; excessive red on the wings of Partridge, Duckwing and Pile females.

Fret Marks   Structural faults on feathers, appearing as transparent lines across (mainly) tail and wing feathers. Black and lavender feathers are often affected, the pigments requiring higher than normal levels of certain vitamins when feathers are growing.

Gay   Oversized white spots on the tips of feathers in Black Mottled, Millefleurs and some other plumage patterns. These spots are small and neat on one-year-old birds, getting progressively larger with each annual moult.

Ground Colour   The background colour of plumage patterns.

Gypsy Face   Dark facial skin (maroon or very dark blue) required on some varieties, a fault on others.

Hackles   Long, pointed feathers on the neck of both sexes of chickens, and the back of males (Saddle Hackles).

Hard-Feather   UK show breed section that includes breeds originally kept for cockfighting and purely exhibition breeds derived from them. They have tight, sleek plumage with little fluff.

Heavy Breed, Soft-Feather   UK show breed section, partly based on weight, partly on origin. The smaller Heavy Breeds and the larger Light Breeds are about the same weights. The miniature versions of large Heavy Breeds are **Heavy Breed Soft-Feather Bantams**.

Hen   A female after its first adult moult, about 18 months old.

Henny-Feathered or Hen-Cock   A male with female type (and pattern when applicable) plumage. Characteristic of Campines, Sebrights, pullet-breeder Pencilled Hamburghs and a few others.

Hock   Leg joint at the top of the shank (the scaled part of the leg).

Horn Comb   Type of comb consisting of two fleshy points. Seen (with crest) on Sultans.

Hybrid   Commercial broilers, layers and turkeys bred by crossing (secret!) inbred strains that are retained by breeding companies. They are fertile, and can be bred from by hobbyists, but the resulting youngsters would not grow or lay to poultry industry requirements.

Inbreeding   Mating related animals or birds together. A **Closed flock** can be kept going without ill-effects for many years if there is a fairly large population. Uniformly good quality show stock can be bred this way, so fanciers sometimes work together to avoid very close matings.

Keel   The blade part of the breast bone. **Bent keel** is a deformity caused by young birds using narrow perches.

Lacing A plumage pattern. *See* photos of Sebrights and Laced Wyandotte.

Leader The pointed hind part of a rose comb.

Light Breed, Soft-Feather UK show breed section. Miniature versions of large Light Breeds are **Light Breed Soft-Feather Bantams**.

Line Breeding An early stage of inbreeding (*see* above), when maximum use is made of a few exceptionally good birds, eventually leading to a closed flock being established.

Litter Bedding material, usually straw or wood shavings, on poultry house floors. Except for white-plumaged show birds, it does not need to be replaced very often as long as it is kept dry.

Lopped Comb A comb that flops over to one side. A show fault on many breeds, but desired on single-combed Ancona, Leghorn, Minorca and some other females. The males of these breeds usually have upright (correct for showing) combs for a few months, which eventually 'go over', after which they are kept at home for breeding.

Mealy or Mealiness Fine white spotting (as if dusted with flour), a fault on Black and Buff birds.

Mossy or Mossiness Fine black spotting, a fault on some plumage patterns – for example, the centres of laced feathers.

Mottled Plumage pattern with white spots on the ends of feathers. *See* photo of Ancona.

Outbreeding Mating unrelated birds of the same breed. It improves general health, laying and so on, but can ruin intricate plumage patterns and make the smaller bantam breeds grow too large.

Partridge Two different plumage patterns, which have the same name. The males of both are very similar Black-reds, it is the females that differ. One type can be seen in the Partridge Modern Game bantam photo, the other in the Partridge Cochin photo. Such historical anomalies often confuse beginners, but just have to be learnt.

Pea Comb or Triple Comb   Comb type resembling three small single combs fused together, the name being derived from its supposed resemblance to an open pod of peas. Seen on Brahmas, Indian Game/Cornish and others.

Pearl Eye   White or yellow iris colour required on Asil, Malay, Shamo and others.

Pencilled   Two different plumage patterns that by historical chance have the same name. *See* photo of Pencilled Hamburgh and Dark Brahma female, the latter's pattern being called Silver Pencilled on Plymouth Rocks and Wyandottes. Silver Pencilled Hamburghs have the same pattern as the Gold Pencilled Hamburg pictured, but in black and white.

Peppering   Fine, random, black peppering on the back and wings of Partridge and Duckwing females.

Pile or Pyle   A plumage pattern in which the black parts of the Black-red/Partridge (as Modern Game) pattern are white instead.

Point-of-lay   A pullet when she is just about to start laying. Hybrid layers reach this stage at 18–20 weeks of age, but many pure breeds are 30 weeks or older before they lay. Do not change pure breeds from growers' to layers' pellets until they appear mature, whatever it says on the bag!

Primaries   The outer ten main flight feathers on the wing.

Pullet   A young female fowl, up to her first adult moult (about 18 months old), when she is a hen.

Pullet Breeder   *See* Double Mating.

Rare Breed   A UK show breed section. Breeds that are covered by the Rare Poultry Society because they do not have their own separate breed club in the UK. It is a practical definition for show administration purposes as it is impossible to keep track of breed populations.

Reachy   Tall and upright carriage, desired on some breeds (for example, Modern Game), a fault on breeds that should stand in a more horizontal, sedate manner.

Roach Back   A deformed, humped back. Not to be confused with the desired curved back of Malays and the very rare Bergische Kräher, bred for cock-crowing competitions for centuries in a small district in Germany.

Rose Comb   Low comb type, the top surface of which is covered with small points ('workings'). The Rosecomb (written as one word) Bantam breed obviously has a rose comb.

Saddle or Saddle Hackles   Long, pointed feathers on the back of all male fowl, except for the few Henny or Hen-cock varieties.

Sappiness   Faulty yellowish tinge on white plumage, almost identical to Brassiness, but in this case caused by eating excess grass or maize when moulting. Exhibitors of white varieties restrict access to both at this time.

Secondaries   The inner set of main wing flight feathers.

Self Colour   Plumage of one colour all over – for example, Black, Buff and White varieties of many breeds.

Serrations   The 'saw-toothed' top part of a single comb.

Shafty   Having the central shaft (stem) of feathers a lighter colour than the rest of the feather. Desirable on Dark Dorking and Welsummer females, a fault on Buff breeds as it detracts from the even colour required.

Side Sprig   Spikes growing on the side (towards the back) of single combs. A show disqualifying fault on every single-combed breed except the very rare Penedesenca, which must have a large sprig on each side.

Spangled   Two plumage patterns that historically have the same name. *See* photo of Silver Spangled Hamburgh and Spangled Old English Game bantams.

Splash   Mostly white plumage with irregular black and blue markings. A by-product of breeding Blues. Splashes may be useful for breeding, but are not usually shown.

Split Wing   A gap between the primary and secondary sets of flight feathers seen when the wing is opened. A show disqualification with all breeds except Ko-Shamo and its relations. Juvenile plumage is rather narrow, so many young birds appear to have split wing, but are sound when they have their adult plumage.

Squirrel Tail   Very high tail carriage, held towards the head. A serious show fault on all breeds except Japanese (Chabo) bantams.

Strain   A carefully bred flock, all birds more or less related to each other, within a variety.

Trio   A male and two females, the traditional unit of pure breeds. There are also competitive classes for matching trios at shows. A good uniform strain will be needed to win these classes.

Type   General breed characteristic shape of body, leg length, tail formation and so on.

Undercolour   Colour of the fluff and lower part of feathers, only seen when lifted. An important judging point with Buff and Barred breeds, where the colour/barring must go down to the skin.

Variety   There are several varieties of most breeds – for example, large Barred, bantam Buff.

Vulture Hocks   Stiff feathers growing down from the hock joint of some feather-footed breeds – for example, Booted bantams and Sultans.

Walnut Comb   Comb type consisting of a compact fleshy lump on males, virtually no comb at all on females. Seen on Kraienköppes, Malays and Orloffs.

Wattles   The two fleshy laps below the beak of most breeds of fowl.

Wing Bar   A line of differently coloured feathers across the middle of the wings of males in some plumage patterns. This band is glossy blue-black on Duckwing males, its supposed similarity to the wing band on wild Mallard drakes being the origin of this variety's name.

Wing Bay   The triangular (when the wing is folder) lower part of the wing. It is bay (reddish brown – ref. bay horses) on Black-red males, but the term is used for this part of the wing on all colour varieties.

Wing Bow   The upper or 'shoulder' part of the wing.

Wry Tail   A deformity where the tail is permanently held to one side. It is often associated with back deformities.

White Japanese Chabo Bantams by C.S.Th. Van Gink.

Further Reading

All published in UK unless otherwise stated. In addition to these, many of the poultry books published in the nineteenth century are still very useful, as well as being valuable collector's items. You may be lucky enough to find some of them in secondhand/antiquarian bookshops or on the internet.

American Poultry Association, *The American Standard of Perfection*, USA, 1985 and other editions.

Anderson Brown, A.F., *The Incubation Book*, 1979 and later editions.

Batty, Joseph & Bleazard, J.P., *Understanding Modern Game*, 1976.

Batty, Joseph, *Lewis Wright and His Poultry*, 1983, 2001.

Brown, Edward, *Races of Domestic Poultry*, 1906 (reprinted 1985 and subsequently).

Carefoot, Dr W.C., *Creative Poultry Breeding*, 1985, 2005.

Entwisle, William Flamark, *Bantams*, 1894 (reprinted 1981 and subsequently).

Hawkey, K.J.C., *Understanding Indian Game*, 1978.

Houghton-Wallace, Janice, *Not Just for Christmas – A Complete Guide to Raising Turkeys*, 2007.

House, Charles Arthur, *Leghorn Fowls*, 1927 (UK), 2007 (New Zealand).

Jeffrey, Fred P., *Bantam Breeding and Genetics*, 1977 (other editions: *Bantam Chickens*, USA).

Jeffrey, Fred P. (ed.), *Wynadotte Bantams*, 1984 (USA).

Kay, Ian, *Stairway to the Breeds*, 1997.

Palin, John K., *Understanding Japanese Bantams*, 1980.

Poultry Club of Great Britain, *British Poultry Standards*, 1997.

Scrivener, David, *Starting with Bantams*, 2002.

Scrivener, David, *Exhibition Poultry Keeping*, 2005.

Scrivener, David, *Rare Poultry Breeds*, 2006.

Silk, William Henry, *Bantams and Miniature Fowl*, 1951 and later editions.

Verhof, Esther & Rijs, Aad, *The Complete Encyclopedia of Chickens*, The Netherlands, 2003, 2006.

Index